FEE MINING ADVENTURES
&
ROCK HUNTING EXPEDITIONS
IN
THE U.S.

By
James Martin Monaco
&
Jeannette Hathaway Monaco

Published by: **GEM GUIDES BOOK CO.**
315 Cloverleaf Drive, Suite F
Baldwin Park, CA 91706

Copyright © 1997 Gem Guides Book Co.

Printed and bound in the United States of America

Cover Design: Mark Webber

Library of Congress Catalog Number: 96-79642
ISBN 0-935182-92-6

DISCLAIMER:
    Due to the possibility of personal error, typographical error, misinterpretation of information, and the many changes due to man or nature, *Fee Mining Adventures & Rock Hunting Expeditions in the U.S.*, its publisher and all other persons directly or indirectly associated with this publication assume no responsibility for accidents, injury or any losses by individuals or groups using this publication.
    In rough terrain and hazardous areas all persons are advised to be aware of possible changes due to man or nature that occur at the various collecting sites.

"THERE IS SOMETHING ABOUT TREASURE THAT
FASTENS ITSELF UPON A MAN'S MIND. HE WILL PRAY AND
BLASPHEME AND STILL PERSEVERE, AND WILL CURSE THE
DAY HE HEARD OF IT, AND WILL LET HIS LAST HOUR COME
UPON HIM UNAWARES, STILL BELIEVING THAT HE MISSED
IT BY ONLY A FOOT."

-JOSEPH CONRAD-

Good luck hunting for your treasure. May this book be a resource
to aid your search.

— Jenny & Jim Monaco —

INTRODUCTION

We have always enjoyed traveling and treasure hunting. We have panned for gold, dug for precious stones and searched beaches for Spanish treasure, meeting great people everywhere we go. However, there have been many times when after a trip, we discovered that we were within minutes of a place to mine and we were unaware it existed. It frustrated us to no end to miss opportunities to enjoy our hobby. Another frustration was to travel to a gold-bearing area of California only to find what seemed to be every square inch of territory covered with mining claim posters. We decided to search for a source book that would help us find places to treasure hunt and rock collect. To date, we have not found that book. So, we did the next best thing — we wrote one ourselves. Now you and your family won't miss an opportunity by a few miles without knowing of its existence.

There are over a hundred places for you to go and try your luck on your own adventure. We are certain that we have only scratched the surface. At the end of this book there is a page for you to help us make additions to a future edition. If you know of a mine we have left out, drop us a note and we'll add it to the next edition.

Some places listed are best suited to beginners. They have instructors, equipment rentals and help for you when you need it. They are established mines with reliable, helpful, experienced staff. We like these places because you can go and get help if you need it. They are well suited to families. There are people around with whom you can swap stories and specimens.

Some of the places listed are wild and isolated. These locations are better suited to prospectors with experience and their own equipment. They are off the beaten path and offer opportunities to enjoy the outdoors undisturbed.

This book is intended as a resource for your next trip. Pack up your car or mobile home and plan an adventure. Many places allow you to camp right at the mine. Mining and collecting sites are organized to give you a good idea of what each establishment has to offer. Choose the ones that best fit your level of hunting. We have included brief information on the mine and what equipment you need to bring. PLEASE CALL AHEAD TO BE SURE THE ESTABLISHMENT WILL BE OPEN DURING THE TIME YOU PLAN TO VISIT.

We hope this guidebook will become a valuable resource to you, and that you and your family will have wonderful adventures together. We are planning a trip across North America in the near future. We will be using our own book as a reference. Maybe we will see you at some of the mines. Best of luck in your search.

TRIP PLANNING

Anyone who plans to visit any of these locations for the purpose of collecting or mining is advised to call ahead to make reservations and verify that the mine is open. Some locations open and close based on the weather or snow cover. It is always a good idea to check before you make the trip.

Always let a friend know exactly where you plan to go and when you plan to return. Be sure to check in when you get back. This is always a good idea and an especially important practice when searching in a remote area of the country. If your search takes you off the beaten path or into an area of the country with which you are unfamiliar, do your research. Don't travel alone.

If you need a permit or to gain permission to mine on private land, get it before you venture out. There is nothing as frustrating as getting to your destination without proper permits.

Be sure to bring a stocked first aid kit with you to care for cuts and bruises. In some areas of the country a snake bite kit is recommended. As with any form of exercise, it is wise to check with your physician before undertaking a strenuous outing.

Be familiar with local plants and animals, weather conditions and climate. All this information will help you to be better prepared and insure a safe, productive expedition.

Check that you have packed the proper tools and equipment for your adventure. Include eye protection for mining that requires the use of hammers or chisels. Pack work gloves to keep your hands from blistering. The clothes you choose to pack will depend on the season, climate and terrain in which you will mine.

There are some items that are needed for most trips. Bring a hat, sturdy boots and comfortable clothes. Long pants will protect your legs from brush and other hazards. Take bug spray and sun screen with you. Bring clothing for changes in temperature and weather. Dress in layers so you can remove your windbreaker, sweater, sweatshirt or vest as the day or you heat up. Older clothing is preferable since it may get stained. A rain poncho should be in your standard equipment, as well as a clean change of clothing, socks and a towel. Dry, clean clothes cheer the spirit, soothe the soul and make the ride home more bearable.

Some locations require only a swimsuit and towel, while other locations may require a wet suit and scuba tank, so check with your destination for details.

Many mines provide food and drink. Others do not. It is wise to always carry drinking water with you, especially if you are traveling in desert areas. Pack plenty of food. Physical labor builds a big appetite!

Now you need to pack your tools. The following list consists of the standard tools you will need for almost all of your adventures. This list is meant to help you get organized.

STANDARD TOOLS:
   Shovel
   Five-gallon bucket
   Small trowel and hand garden tools
   Crowbar / Prybar
   Eye Protection (goggles)
   Screwdriver
   Rock hammer
   Pick
   Sledgehammer
   Work gloves
   Closable plastic container
Some mines require specialized equipment. Whenever possible we have tried to include that information with the listing for the individual mine.

ADDITIONAL EQUIPMENT FOR SAPPHIRE / DIAMOND / OPAL MINING:
   Tweezers
   One-eighth-, one-quarter-, and one-half-inch sifting screens
   Plastic spray bottle
   Whisk broom or brush
   Washtub

GOLD MINING TOOLS:
   Gold pan
   Snuffer bottle
   Collecting bottles

ADDITIONAL EQUIPMENT FOR EXPERIENCED GOLD MINERS:
   Sluice box
   High banker
   Dredge
   Metal detector

   If you plan to do any metal detecting, you need to pack your detector, a pouch to hold your finds and some kind of scoop or shovel.
   Many mines can provide all the tools that you will need. Some rent equipment, while still others provide very little. We suggest that you check with the individual mine if you are uncertain of what to bring along.

FOR YOUR SAFETY

To make the most out of your adventure once you get there you need to observe the following words to the wise to give you a leg up on the greenhorns.

1. When swinging rock hammers, sledgehammers or a pick make sure everyone is clear of your work area and that you have adequate footing.

2. Never enter caves or old mining tunnels. Snakes love caves for their cool shade. Caves are also frequented by other animals including mountain lions and bears. Old shafts are extremely dangerous and unstable. They are not worth the risk. Never tunnel into banks with overhangs or on cliffs.

3. If you are searching for gold for the first time, try to get a panning lesson. Many mines teach gold panning. You can teach yourself of course, but in our opinion, nothing compares to watching an expert and gaining some real experience.

4. Stay out of fast-moving water. Do not damage or prospect in the riverbank or disturb plant life while mining. Be sure you are not in a flash flood area. Heavy rains upstream can flood downstream in minutes and under a clear blue sky.

5. Check out the plant life on the banks to avoid poison ivy, or other harmful plants.

6. Contain all camp fires in a fire pit.

7. If you are working a dredge, clear all large rocks away from the hole you are working to prevent cave-ins or rock slides. Be careful when digging into a bank that the hole does not collapse. Never work in a hole deeper than you are tall if you are alone.

8. Remember to fill in the holes you dig. Holes are dangerous and unsightly.

9. Watch over children and unexperienced miners. Instruct children on how to use tools. Point out hazards and take frequent breaks.

THE GOLD RUSH OF NORTH AMERICA

The Reed Gold Mine reported the first gold find in the United States. As the story goes, in 1799, Reed's son, Conrad, found a large yellow rock in Little Meadow Creek while playing hooky from church. A silversmith in Concord was unable to identity the rock, but measured it's weight at 17 pounds. The Reeds used it as a door stop until a jeweler bought it for $3.50 in 1802, less than one-tenth of it's value. Later Reed discovered his mistake and "convinced" the jeweler to compensate him. Mining later began by Reed and others and a 28-pound nugget was found. A total of $100,000 worth of gold was unearthed by 1824. North Carolina was the first gold producing state in the U.S.

Gold was discovered in 1806 near Spotsylvania County, Virginia. Several mines were in operation by 1825. Mining ceased in 1849, when the Virginia miners left the state to head for the gold rush in California. In 1850 the production of gold in Virginia was reduced by half because of a labor shortage. Gold was last mined commercially in Virginia in 1947 as a by-product of lead mining.

Gold was also discovered in South Carolina in the early 1800s. Lancaster County was shipping gold to the United States mint in 1829. Mining, interrupted by several wars, continued throughout the 1800s.

Georgia had a gold rush in 1828 which lasted to 1850 with over 4000 miners working the hills. Gold was first discovered in Georgia in 1818, by Mr. Benjamin Hicks, who made the discovery by kicking over a rock to expose a lump of gold the color and size of an egg's yolk. Miners deserted this area, as their counter-parts in Virginia had, when gold was discovered in California. But they came back when California gold ran out in 1855. Mining was again interrupted, this time by the Civil War to be resumed again after the end of the war. Commercial mining of gold continued until World War II.

New Mexico gave the cry of gold in the Ortiz Mountains, south of Santa Fe in 1828. This was not the first gold rush in this area. Spanish conquistadors discovered and mined gold here after searching throughout South America and Mexico. Prior to that Native Americans mined gold here for unknown periods of time.

Alabama had it's own gold rush beginning in the 1830s. Gold was discovered in Tennessee in 1831 on the Ococee Land District which belonged to the Cherokees. The land was taken along with the gold. The most famous area here was Cokercreek which is still producing gold today.

In 1838 gold was found in Ohio where is was deposited 14,000 years earlier during the glacier's retreat. The origin of this gold was probably somewhere in Northern Canada.

The largest gold rush in North America occurred in 1849 in California. Gold had been discovered a year earlier at Sutter's Saw Mill by a worker named James W. Marshall. In January of 1848 a dam was built on the American River. Water was channeled to the dam to remove the loose dirt and gravel and then turned off again.

On Monday, January 24, 1848, James Marshall walked in the channel and spotted grains of shiny metal the size of wheat. Suspecting this was gold he rushed to tell his fellow workers that he had found a gold mine. Captain John Sutter was informed of the potential find and did all within his power to prevent this story from leaking out, while buying as much surrounding land from the Native Americans as possible. The remoteness of the area slowed the speed of the discovery.

In March of 1848 gold was mined and the discovery reported in the San Francisco newspapers. Soon men from around the world began to migrate to Coloma, California to establish the first mining camp. John Sutter was there to sell supplies, food, tools and claims to the would-be miners.

In the fall of 1849 the number of miners in California had forever changed the population distribution in the United States. Men worked in groups, mining an area until the gold disappeared. The miners then moved up the creeks and rivers to search for other gold deposits. Camp towns sprung up overnight, to disappear just as quickly. Many of these towns are well preserved and still exist along Highway 49. Their names create vivid images; Fiddletown, Rough and Ready, Chinese Camp, Sutters Creek, Placerville and Gold Run, to name a few. In 1853, at least 65 million dollars worth of gold was taken from California mines. Mining in California continued until the surface gold played out in 1855.

During the same time period gold was discovered in Alaska at Kenai River in 1848 by a Russian Mining Engineer. Alaska did not become a United States territory until March 30, 1867. Alaska had a series of strikes or rushes in Anchorage, Nome and Fairbanks. Gold continues to be discovered today in Alaska.

Nevada was found to have gold in 1849. During the gold mining process much blue clay was uncovered and discarded. This clay was later found to be rich in silver. Silver became the true treasure of Nevada.

The western states were next searched for gold and silver. It was found in 1852 in Idaho, Montana and Oregon, in Washington in 1853 and Utah in 1858. That same year gold miners in Arizona were earning $4.00 to $150.00 dollars a day.

In 1859, the slogan "Pike's Peak or Bust" became the cry of gold miners heading for Colorado. Gold production in Colorado reached 40 million troy ounces.

Montana, which had shown some gold in 1852, became the next rush site in 1863, when large quantities of gold were found near Virginia City.

The Black Hills of South Dakota, in and around Rapid City, experienced their own influx of miners for gold betweeen 1876 and 1878.

Gold is still mined commercially in the U.S. and small scale miners are still out there even as you read this, with picks, shovels, dredges and sluice boxes looking for that precious metal.

TABLE OF CONTENTS

TABLE OF CONTENTS cont.

TABLE OF CONTENTS cont.

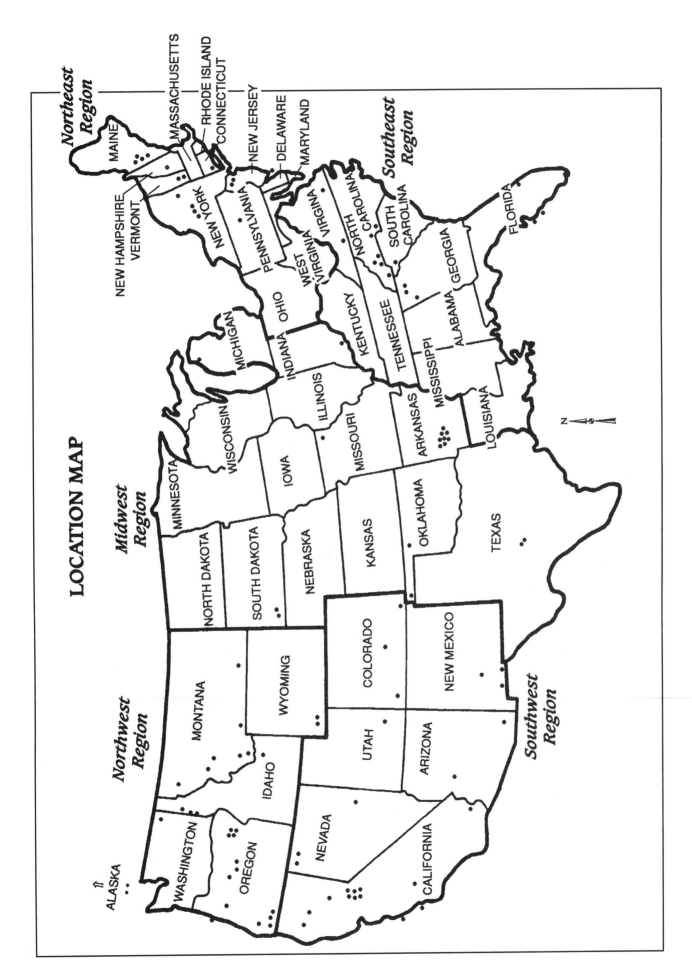

LOCATION MAP

Northeast Region

Southeast Region

Midwest Region

Northwest Region

Southwest Region

MAINE
NEW HAMPSHIRE
VERMONT
MASSACHUSETTS
RHODE ISLAND
CONNECTICUT
NEW JERSEY
DELAWARE
MARYLAND
NEW YORK
PENNSYLVANIA
WEST VIRGINIA
VIRGINIA
NORTH CAROLINA
SOUTH CAROLINA
GEORGIA
FLORIDA
ALABAMA
MISSISSIPPI
TENNESSEE
KENTUCKY
OHIO
INDIANA
ILLINOIS
MICHIGAN
WISCONSIN
MINNESOTA
IOWA
MISSOURI
ARKANSAS
LOUISIANA
OKLAHOMA
TEXAS
KANSAS
NEBRASKA
SOUTH DAKOTA
NORTH DAKOTA
MONTANA
WYOMING
COLORADO
NEW MEXICO
UTAH
ARIZONA
IDAHO
NEVADA
CALIFORNIA
OREGON
WASHINGTON
ALASKA

N

MAINE

Gold Panning - Swift River Gold Panning Area

REGION:
Northeast

ADDRESS:
Mexico Field Office
149 Main Street
Mexico, Maine 04257
(207) 369-0731

SEASON:
Summer and fall

HOURS:
Daylight

COST:
Free

DIRECTIONS:
From Coos Canyon Picnic Area on State Highway 17 in Byron, drive 1.7 miles north and east on Byron Road toward Tumbledown Mountain. Turn left onto the unpaved road. Take the fork to the right and cross the branch of the Swift River. Park your car on either side of the road after crossing the bridge.

WHAT TO BRING:
Gold mining tools including a gold pan, sluice, dredge, bucket, shovel, pick and work gloves.

INFORMATION:
The Swift River is in Byron in Oxford County. You must get permission to prospect by calling or writing the Unit Supervisor at the above address. No state permit is required for small scale mining.

Disturbance to the river bank is prohibited. You may use a pan or sluice or a dredge with up to a four-inch hose diameter. Large scale mining requires a permit from the Maine Department of Enviromental Protection.

Flakes to nuggets have been found in this area, along with other heavy material including almandine garnet, magnetite and staurolite. The area downstream of the parking area has produced gold.

Maine is rivaled only by Florida and Alaska in the size and ferocity of its biting insects. Bring a strong, deep woods bug repellant. Long pants and long-sleeved clothing are suggested.

The Timberlands manager reminds us that deer hunting season is in late November, bow season is earlier. Wear bright clothes or avoid mining during this time. If you do decide to collect during hunting season, keep children and pets close by.

MAINE

*Tourmaline & Garnets -
Bemis Stream Prospect*

REGION:
Northeast

ADDRESS:
Mexico Field Office
149 Main Street
Mexico, Maine 04257
(207) 369-0731

DIRECTIONS:
From the town of Mexico at the junction of U.S. Highway 2 and State Highway 17, drive north 17.1 miles on State Highway 17 to the town of Houghton. Turn left after the field onto the dirt road and cross the bridge at Swift River. Go northwest on the gravel logging road for 6.3 miles from State Highway 17 to the bridge over Bemis Stream. Park on the right.

SEASON:
Summer and fall

HOURS:
Daylight hours

COST:
Free

WHAT TO BRING:
Bring standard mining tools, your own food and plenty to drink. You may also need a quarter-inch screen and a container to hold your finds. Maine is noted for its beautiful woodlands and its huge mosquitoes and biting black flies. A high quality bug spray is recommended.

INFORMATION:
The Bemis Stream location is on federal land. You must call to get permission to prospect here. Only small scale prospecting and personal collecting is permitted. Permission is easily granted. Green tourmaline crystals can be found in the ledge along the river and garnets and other quartz can be found here as well.

MAINE

Beryl, Quartz, Tourmaline - Bumpus Quarry

REGION:
Northeast

ADDRESS:
Rodney Kimball
P.O. Box 121
Bethel, Maine 04217
(207) 836-3945

DIRECTIONS:
The Bumpus Quarry is located in Albany, Maine. You must call Mr. Kimball at his shop to make reservations to visit the quarry. His shop is located on U.S. Highway 2 in West Bethel.

SEASON:
Spring to late fall

HOURS:
Daylight

COST:
Adults — $20.00 per person, depending on number in party
Children under 8 years — free

WHAT TO BRING:
Bring standard mining tools, your own food and plenty to drink.

INFORMATION:
　　The Bumpus Quarry is primarily composed of coarse-grained, light-colored granite. Millions of years ago, when the granite was gradually cooling, rare elements seeped into the fractures in the rock. These elements crystalized to form beryl, quartz, tourmaline, zircon, and garnet deposits. This is a great place to pick up some nice specimens for your collection.

　　This location requires hard rock mining. You will need to break apart rocks found in the open pit dumps or work the quarry walls. Well-formed crystals grow in the granite, tightly encased in the rock matrix. The best crystals are found surrounded by quartz. Quartz is most commonly milky white, smoky gray or black. Look for quartz crystals and gently break away the brittle quartz to expose matrix specimens. Large flat sheets of mica in black and white are also common here.

　　Before heading out please call Mr. Kimball a few days prior to your trip to make reservations.

MAINE

*Aquamarine -
Songo Pond Mine*

REGION:
Northeast

ADDRESS:
Jan Brownstein
P.O. Box 864
Bethel, Maine 04217
(207) 824-3898

DIRECTIONS:
The mine is just south of Bethel, Maine. Take State Highway 5 and follow the signs to the Songo Mine. The mine is 4 miles from Bethel and .25 mile from the State Highway 5 turnoff.

SEASON:
May 1 to October 31,
weather permitting

HOURS:
The mine opens at 9:00 a.m.

COST:
Adults — $10.00
Children (7 to 13 years) — $5.00

WHAT TO BRING:
Bring standard mining tools, your own food and plenty to drink.

INFORMATION:
This is a working mine that is currently in operation mining aquamarine. You must call ahead for an appointment to collect. The mine offers opportunities to watch the operation work. Collectors are permitted to work the tailings pile for aquamarine, apatite, tourmaline, mica, garnet and quartz. Some help is offered to beginners to get you started on the right foot. You may keep all you find, limited to one, five-gallon bucket of material per day.

The mine is located on a hill with a view of Songo Pond on one side and the Sunday River on the other. The tailings pile is usually in full sun, so a hat and sunscreen is recommended. You may drive tools and passengers to the mine, but then you must park in the lot.

NEW HAMPSHIRE

Feldspar & Beryl - Ruggles Mine

REGION:
Northeast

ADDRESS:
Isinglass Mountain
Grafton, New Hampshire
(603) 523-4275

SEASON:
Open weekends, mid-May to mid-June
Open weekdays, mid-June to
mid-October

HOURS:
9:00 a.m. to 5:00 p.m., except July and August when
hours are 9:00 a.m. to 6:00 p.m. The last ticket is sold
one hour before closing.

COST:
Adults — $12.00
Children 4 - 11 — $5.00
This price buys all the rocks you can haul to your car in two trips.

DIRECTIONS:
Ruggles Mine is north and west of Grafton, New Hampshire. Take U.S. Highway 4 west approximately 9 miles, following the signs. Turn onto the mine access road at the sign across from the white church. The access road is unpaved.

WHAT TO BRING:
No tools are necessary to find specimens. You may wish to have a rock hammer and bucket. Some supplies can be rented at the mine. If you want to explore the shallow caves bring a flashlight. A snack bar and picnic tables are available.

INFORMATION:
This mine boasts that 150 minerals can be found here. The most common are mica, feldspar and beryl. This mine is actually the top of a mountain. They suggest you leave trailers at the bottom of the gravel road. The drive up is definately worth the trip. There are spectacular views of the surrounding mountain. The entrance cuts through the mountain, leading you into the quarry. The entire top of the mountain has been mined away and the interior is open to the sky. High pillars of feldspar rise on each side of the entrance like the columns of a Roman temple. There are some small caves that can be explored from the main mining area.

Mica was coveted for its transparence and fire-resistant qualities and was commonly used for lanterns and stove windows. It is still used today in the cosmetics industry to make lipstick glitter. Feldspar is also used in many products, as you will see if you visit the mine. Visitors can take a walking tour of the mine's history, starting outside the mines entrance in the museum.

VERMONT

Gold Panning - Camp Plymouth State Park

REGION:
Northeast

ADDRESS:
Camp Plymouth State Park
Route 1, Box 489
Ludlow, Vermont   05149
(802) 228-2025

SEASON:
Memorial Day weekend to August 30

HOURS:
10:00 a.m. until dusk

COST:
Adults — $2.00
Children — $1.50

DIRECTIONS:
From Ludlow, Vermont take State Highway 100 north. Turn right at the Echo Lake Inn where the sign points to Camp Plymouth State Park. Drive 1.5 miles around the lake and take the first left at the sign to Camp Plymouth State Park. The park is .5 mile after the left turn.

WHAT TO BRING:
Gold mining equipment and bug spray. May is blackfly season in Vermont.

INFORMATION:
The first gold found in Vermont was found in Buffalo Brook in what is now Camp Plymouth State Park. A gold nugget was found by an unknown fisherman in 1826 and the search for gold was on in Vermont. By 1885 the cost of mining was more than the gold yielded here and commercial mining ceased. If you walk a half mile up the Echo Lake Overlook trail you can see the remains of a old collapsed air shaft, off to your left after the walkover bridge. This is all that remains of the gold mine. Buffalo Brook is on your right and this is where panning is permitted.

The park allows gold dredging and gold mining without permit, but you will need to call ahead to notify the ranger station prior to your arrival. You may also metal detect for nuggets, but no artifacts may be removed, according to Vermont state law. Dredging requires a state permit be obtained by writing or calling the Stream Alteration Engineer, State of Vermont, Water Quality Division, 450 Asa Bloomer State Office Building, Rutland, Vermont 05701, (802) 786-5906.

The walls of the brook are steep. Bedrock is exposed in some places along the brook and the brook is very shallow in other places. Much of the gold found here is fine flakes, but a few nuggets have been reported. Vermont has some native gold, however, most of the gold here was deposited by glaciers during the last ice age.

VERMONT

*Gold Panning -
Richard's Gold Mine*

REGION:
Northeast

ADDRESS:
1944 Main Street
Athol, Massachusetts 01331
(508) 249-7736

DIRECTIONS:
The Richard's Gold Mine is located in Ludlow, Vermont. Reservations are required and directions are given at that time.

SEASON:
May to October, weather permitting

HOURS:
11:00 a.m. to 5:00 p.m.

COST:
$25.00 per person per day
$15.00 per person per day with groups of nine or more

WHAT TO BRING:
You will be supplied with everything you need to pan for gold including gold pans, vials to hold your finds, shovels and picks. There are no food or drinks available at the mine so bring them with you.

INFORMATION:
Richard's Gold Mine was first worked in the late 1890s, when gold was discovered by a prospector returning from the California gold fields. Mining operations were conducted through the 1940s. Large amounts of placer gold and nuggets were collected.

During World War II, the War Powers Act closed all mines not essential to the war effort. This act also made it illegal for foreigners to own mines in the United States. This forced the Canadian owner to abandon his mine.

The mine is located in the central Green Mountain area. Gold found here ranges from small nuggets to gold dust. Only gold panning is permitted. You may not use dredges or other mining tools. Richard's offers gold panning classes, trips and lectures.

NEW YORK

Herkimer Diamonds - Ace of Diamonds Mine

REGION:
Northeast

ADDRESS:
State Highway 28
Middleville, New York 13406
(315) 891-3855 or 866-3900

SEASON:
April to November 1

HOURS:
9:00 a.m. to 5:00 p.m.

COST:
Adults — $5.00
Children — $2.00

DIRECTIONS:
The Ace of Diamonds Mine is located on State Highway 28, 8 miles north of Herkimer. Herkimer, New York, is Exit 30 off the New York State Thruway/ Interstate 90.

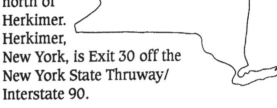

WHAT TO BRING:
Bring standard mining tools, including sledgehammers, safety goggles, wedges, and gloves. Tools are also available for rent or for sale at the office. Tools are helpful, but you can find crystals without them. Bring your own food and plenty to drink. Picnic tables are available.

INFORMATION:
You can dig your own Herkimer diamonds here. These doubly-terminated, clear, quartz crystals are found in their natural state looking like cut diamonds. The "diamonds" are found inside pockets in rocks, loose on the ground or by working the cliff wall. Children will have better luck in the tailings piles. A keen eye can find "diamonds" anywhere on the ground, especially after a rain.

Some miners stay for weeks and slowly work at taking down a section of cliff face using nothing but hand tools (wedges, sledgehammers, crowbars and prybars). They must take the wall down from the top to reach the diamond layer, removing somewhere between 10 and 30 feet of stone.

Many day miners find likely rocks on the large tailings piles and spend the day breaking open rocks with hand sledges. Others just turn over rocks to find the diamond beneath. Lastly, miners use screens, garden rakes and the naked eye to search the earth for loose crystals. Crystals can be as large as four inches, but you will have to "work the wall" and be very lucky to find one of these. The average crystal is a quarter- to a half-inch long and breathtakingly beautiful.

Camping is available both at the mine or at a KOA Campground directly across the road.

NEW YORK

Herkimer Diamonds - Herkimer Diamond Mine

REGION:
Northeast

ADDRESS:
5661 State Route 5
Herkimer, New York 13350
(315) 891-7355

SEASON:
April 1 to December 1,
weather permitting
Camping: April to November

HOURS:
9:00 a.m. to 5:00 p.m.

COST:
Adults — $6.00
Children — $5.00
Admission includes a visit to the rock museum

DIRECTIONS:
Take the New York State Thruway (I-90) to Exit 30 to State Highway 28. The mine is 7 miles north of Herkimer on State Highway 28.

WHAT TO BRING:
Bring standard mining tools, your own food and plenty to drink. A plastic container with a lid, goggles and a large bucket are highly recommended. The mine will let you borrow hammers, chisels and goggles in exchange for your driver's license.

INFORMATION:
These double-terminated, clear, quartz crystals are found in their natural state looking like cut diamonds. Diamond hunting can be hard work. The "diamonds" are found inside air pockets in the local stone. They can be found by turning over rocks in the tailings piles, breaking open likely rocks with hammers or working the cliff wall. Children will have better luck in the tailings piles. A keen eye can find "diamonds" anywhere on the ground. The people at the mine are friendly and helpful in orienting you. The best candidate rocks are the ones with the dark black pockets visible on the rocks exterior. You can take as many host rocks and diamonds home with you as you find, no limit.

There is a playground, picnic tables, and a rock and gift shop here. Included with your admission price is a trip to their museum, located above the large rock shop. Across the street from the mine is a KOA campsite on the river. It has a pool and some cabins, a bathhouse, playground and store. Fly fishing is another popular hobby in this area.

NEW YORK

*Herkimer Diamonds -
Crystal Grove Diamond
Mine & Campground*

REGION:
Northeast

ADDRESS:
161 County Highway 114
St. Johnsville, New York 13452
(518) 568-2914 or (800) KRY-DIAM

SEASON:
April 15 to October 15

HOURS:
8:00 a.m. until dusk

COST:
Adults — $4.00
Children under 14 — $2.50

DIRECTIONS:
Traveling west on the New York State Thruway (I-90) take Exit 29 (westbound) and turn right onto State Highway 10. Then take State Highway 5 west and proceed to St. Johnsville, New York. Turn right onto Division Street at the town's only traffic light. Drive .5 mile and bear right at the fork. Travel 4 miles to the campsite.

WHAT TO BRING:
Standard mining equipment is suggested, along with tweezers, safety goggles and a plastic container with a lid. You may also want a large bucket for carrying home host rocks with good possibilities. Some tools are also available for rent.

INFORMATION:
There are three mines on this property. Herkimer diamonds can be found in the matrix (rock) or by sifting through the earth. Finding these gems involves breaking up the gray host rock with a rock hammer or sledgehammer. Some rocks are barren, without crystal pockets. Look for stones that have existing, empty, visable pockets on their exterior. The pockets you are looking for are black, dark gray or may glitter with drusy quartz. Pockets lined with white, cubed crystals usually are not hosts to diamonds.

Try to bust open the rock. If it doesn't split with four or five good strikes, it may not have any air pockets, so try again with another likely rock. The best time to go to a Herkimer Diamond mine is after a good rain. The crystals are exposed and lie glittering on the soil's surface until they dry, becoming invisible once again. Some miners perfer to use a sifting screen to find crystals. Simply shovel small amounts of earth into a screen and see what you find.

Crystal Grove has camping and tent sites by a trout stream, and motor home sites in a wooded area. The camp has a shop selling groceries, rocks and gifts.

NEW YORK

Garnets -
The Barton Mine

REGION:
Northeast

ADDRESS:
Bonnie Barton
c/o Gore Mineral Shop
P.O. Box 30
North River, New York 12853
(518) 251-2706
(518) 798-5462, off season

SEASON:
Seven days a week beginning the last
weekend in June to Labor Day.
Weekends Labor Day to Columbus Day.

HOURS:
9:00 a.m. to 5:00 p.m.,
Monday - Saturday
11:00 a.m. to 5:00 p.m., Sunday

DIRECTIONS:
Take Interstate 87 to
Exit 23. Then follow
U.S. Highway 9
through
Warrens-
burg. Go
left onto
State Highway 28 for ap-
proximately 21 miles to North
River General Store. Proceed left
up the hill (Gore Mountain) on the paved
Barton Mines Road for 5 miles to the
Barton Mineral Shop on the right-hand
side of the road.

COST:
$3.00 per person
Garnets can be purchased by the pound at a reasonable price.

WHAT TO BRING:
The mine will give you a paper bag for garnets. Bring a plastic bag or small pail to
carry your stones. You may find a garden rake and spray bottle helpful in your
search. Picnic tables are available, bring your own food.

INFORMATION:
This is a tour of a now inactive garnet mine. At one time, this mine produced
gem-quality stones. Some garnets were used to make garnet sandpaper and emery
boards. Garnets were discovered in the Hudson River, near it's source in the Adiron-
dack Mountains in New York. The garnet trail was followed up North River to it's
source on Gore Mountain. Several old quarries remain at this location.
Your visit will begin at the gift shop and headquarters, on top of Gore Mountain.
The drive is steep and the road is unpaved. Unless weather conditions are bad, you
will have no trouble driving up. From the shop you will follow the tour guide in a car
caravan to the quarry. The tour takes place in an open garnet quarry. It includes a
brief history of the mine, some geology and 30 minutes of time to gather garnets.
The stones are plentiful and easy to find. This is ideal for children.

CONNECTICUT

Garnets - Green's Garnet Farm

REGION:
Northeast

ADDRESS:
Perkins Road
Southbury, Connecticut 06488
(203) 264-3550; Call in the evenings

DIRECTIONS:
Green's Garnet Farm is in Southbury, Connecticut, west of Waterbury. From Interstate 84 east, take Exit 15 (Southbury). Then follow State Highway 67 northwest to Roxbury, approximately 8 miles. In Roxbury there is a triangle of grass with a flag pole where several roads meet. Turn left onto South Street, across from the white Episcopal Church. Travel 4.4 miles on South Street to the top of a hill. Make a left onto Perkins Street. Drive .5 mile to where the pavement ends and the road turns sharply to the left. Drive through the gate to the house.

SEASON:
Open all year round

HOURS:
9:00 a.m. to 5:00 p.m.

COST:
$2.00 per car to park. There is no collecting fee.

WHAT TO BRING:
Bring standard mining tools, your own food and plenty to drink.

INFORMATION:
The garnets found here are well-formed, dodecahedron crystals of a dark red or purple color. Some garnets are of gem quality and can be faceted into jewelry. The majority are dark and opaque.

Garnets are plentiful at the farm, making it a favorite spot for local rockhounds. The Archibalds are very casual about allowing collectors onto their property. You can collect all day and there is no limit on the number of garnets you carry out.

The terrain is rocky and there are some cliffs and lots of holes; watch you step. Fill in all holes you make and carry out all your trash. Garnets can be found by raking or screening through loose dirt. Many stones are exposed through the weathering process of the host rock. The more ambitious miner can break large rocks or cliff face to uncover garnets. This involves climbing and using a sledgehammer and chisels.

NEW JERSEY  *Fluorescent Minerals - Sterling Hill Mine & Museum*

REGION:
Northeast

ADDRESS:
30 Plant Street
Ogdensburg, New Jersey 07439
(201) 209-7212

DIRECTIONS:
The Sterling Hill Mine is located a short distance from either Sparta or Franklin, New Jersey off of County Road 517. Take County Road 517 to Ogdensburg and turn north onto Passaic Avenue, driving .7 mile to the entrance to the mine.

SEASON:
Collecting is allowed the last Sunday of each month during operating season. Tours run daily from April 1 to November 30.

HOURS:
10:00 a.m. - 5:00 p.m.
Tours leave at 11:00 a.m., 1:00 p.m. and 3:00 p.m

COST:
Adults — $8.00
Senior Citizens — $7.00
Children under 17— $5.00

WHAT TO BRING:
No special equipment is needed for the tour. For Sunday collecting bring small buckets, gloves, safety goggles, and a rock hammer. A UV light can be helpful to see which rocks fluoresce.

INFORMATION:
   Sterling Hill is the last operating zinc mine in New Jersey, with underground, ancient mine pits and antique mining equipment. The mine museum has an exhibit hall featuring mining artifacts and rare minerals. Walking tours cover one-fifth of a mile of underground tunnels and last between one-and-a-half to two hours. This method of metal mining is explained as you view tunnels, tools and equipment. Bring a sweater or jacket, as the tunnels are a cool 52 degrees year round. The highlight of the tour is seeing the spectacular red and green minerals fluoresce within the mining tunnels.
   Please call and check on the time and price of collecting. Children must be 13 years of age or older to collect at the mine.

NEW JERSEY  *Fluorescent Minerals - Franklin Mineral Museum & Mine Replica*

REGION:
Northeast

ADDRESS:
Evans Street, P.O. Box 54
Franklin, New Jersey 07416
(201) 827-3481

DIRECTIONS:
Franklin Mineral Museum is located off State Highway 23. From State Highway 23 take Route 631 and follow the signs to the museum.

SEASONS:
April 1 to December 1,
Closed Easter and Thanksgiving.
Open weekends only in March, weather permitting.

HOURS:
10:00 a.m. to 4:00 p.m., Monday - Saturday
12:30 to 4:30 p.m., Sunday

COST:
Tours only: Adults — $4.00
Children — $2.00
Tours and collecting: Adults — $7.00
Children — $3.00

WHAT TO BRING:
Bring standard mining tools, your own food and plenty to drink. An ultraviolet light might be helpful, although one is available at the museum.

INFORMATION:
   The mineral museum is outstanding with over 4200 specimens on display. The collection of flourescent minerals is very impressive. Take note of how the minerals look in regular light so you can try to locate them later in the tailings pile. There is also a collection of fossils, petrified wood, shells and Native American artifacts for your enjoyment.
   Franklin is the site of the former New Jersey Zinc Company. The replica mine displays the equipment and methods used to extract zinc. Collecting is done at the Buckwheat tailings next to the museum. Reservations must be made in advance for group tours.

NEW JERSEY

Cape May Diamonds -
Cape May Public Beach

REGION:
Northeast

ADDRESS:
County Route 606
Cape May, New Jersey 08204
(609) 884-9562, Cape May Welcome Center

DIRECTIONS:
Take the Garden State Parkway south to its end. Follow the signs to Cape May on County Road 606.

SEASON:
Open all year round

HOURS:
Daylight hours

COST:
Free

WHAT TO BRING:
Beach toys, a closed container and a sharp eye are all you will need.

INFORMATION:
Cape May Diamonds are small quartz pebbles that have washed up on the beach. They can be found on several beaches in the area including Lighthouse State Park, Cape May Point and Sunset Beach. Look for transparent stones at these sites. For the best results tumble the stones for three weeks. They can be cut by a lapidary to look just like diamonds. Visit local gift shops to see what can be done with these lovely stones.

Cape May is a pretty Northeast summer get-away. The town is just south of Atlantic City and Wildwood, New Jersey. This village has a different look than most resort towns. No highrises. Guesthouses with gingerbread wood trim prevail. The shopping area is touristy, but nice. From Sunset Beach you will see what looks like the remains of a cement building in the ocean. It is actually an experimental cement ship that was constructed during World War II. The ship sailed, but ran aground in a storm and remains where it struck the bottom.

If you tire of the peace and quiet of Cape May, Wildwood is a hop, skip and a jump away. This summer mecca has a large boardwalk, which has carnival-style rides, food, shops and fun. Lots of hustle and bustle and action to be found here, along with a very nice beach. Bring your metal detector!

MARYLAND

Arrowheads & Fossils -
Calvert Cliffs State Park

REGION:
Northeast

ADDRESS:
Point Lookout State Park
P.O. Box 48
Scotland, Maryland 20687
(301) 872-5688

DIRECTIONS:
Driving from Prince Frederick, Maryland, take State Highway 4 south approximatley 14 miles. Follow the signs to Calvert Cliffs State Park.

To fossil hunt follow the signs to the park from State Highway 4 but turn left onto County Road 765 rather than into the main park entrance. Drive .5 mile, just past the Chapel and turn right onto Camp Canoy Road. Continue along the paved road, bearing right when the road changes to dirt. About .25 mile along the dirt road you will come upon the entrance to Bay Breeze on the right. The combination lock code is 1224. After passing through the gate drive ahead to the parking area.

SEASON:
Open all year

HOURS:
Sunrise to sunset, Monday through Saturday

COST:
A nominal entrance fee is charged for entrance to the park.

WHAT TO BRING:
You will be hunting in the water and by the shore so wear a swimsuit or bring a change of clothes because you will get wet. Bring hand tools and a water scoop.

INFORMATION:
Calvert Cliffs are 600-feet high and 30-miles long, rising from the western shores of the Chesapeake Bay. Generations of sea life lived and died here, sinking to the ocean floor to fossilize. These fossils are now exposed by wind and rain. Approximately 600 species have been identified here, among them oysters, clams, scallops and shark's teeth.

To find fossils hike a little under two miles from the parking lot to the cliffs. Fossils can be found on the beach, near the shoreline and in the water. Use a water scoop to improve your chances. You may keep whatever you find. Access to the base of the cliffs is closed to hunting because of frequent landslides.

PENNSYLVANIA

*Quartz Crystals -
Crystal Point
Diamond Mine*

REGION:
Northeast

ADDRESS:
c/o Raytowne
Box 1, 1307 Park Avenue
Williamsport, Pennsylvania 17701
(717) 322-4641

DIRECTIONS:
Take U.S. Highway 15 north from Interstate 80 to Williamsport. Head into Williamsport on Fourth Street west to Rose Street. Turn right onto Rose Street and travel two blocks north to Park Avenue. Stop at the large brick buildings of Raytowne on the right just past Cemetery Street. Raytowne is a converted factory, that is now a dance club and shopping center. From here you will follow the owner, Mr. Smith, down a rough jeep trail to the mine.

SEASON:
May 1 to October 31, depending on the weather

HOURS:
8:00 a.m. to 5:00 p.m., by appointment only

COST:
$30.00 for Adults
$10.00 for Children under 12 years of age

WHAT TO BRING:
Bring basic collecting tools and your own food and drink.

INFORMATION:
   Quartz crystals found here vary in size from small, half-inch crystals to 50-pound crystal clusters. A 200-yard-long trench has been dug, 12-feet deep, to expose the quartz vein without damaging the crystal deposits. Crystals can be dug using picks, shovels and other hand tools. Bring a bucket and gloves. The crystals found are often clear, but sometimes smoky, orange, or pale yellow. Larger crystals are single-terminated crystals. Smaller crystals may be double terminated.
   Mr. Smith tells us that you need to work carefully. Crystals are easily damaged by picks and shovels. A small garden claw or screwdriver are recommended for searching the red clay for crystals. Patience may be rewarded by the discovery of large, whole crystals.

VIRGINIA

Beryl & Smoky Quartz -
Deck Boyles Farm
& Mine

REGION:
Southeast

ADDRESS:
13001 Butlers Road
Amelia, Virginia   23002
(804) 561-2395

DIRECTIONS:
From Amelia, Virginia, take Route 628/Bulters Road approximately 3 miles. Look for mailbox #13001 on the right as the marker for the Boyles Farm and Mine.

SEASON:
Open all year round

HOURS:
Daylight

COST:
$3.00 per day

WHAT TO BRING:
You need standard mining equipment, a lunch and plenty to drink.

INFORMATION:
The mine was first worked during the Civil War when prospectors looking for mica also came across green crystals of beryl. Mica was mined for it's resistance to heat and transparency and was sometimes used in stoves and lanterns instead of glass. Mica is plentiful here.

The elusive and valuable beryl is more difficult to unearth. You may dig all day and only find a piece or two. Beryl unearthed can be as fine as pencil lead. Large specimens of up to an inch in diameter and several inches long have also been found. Blue-green hexagonal crystals are found with the black mica in the red clay soil of the 50-foot pit mine.

Beryl comes in a variety of colors. The beryl family includes tourmaline, emerald and aquamarine. The color of the beryl found here includes clear, gray, gray-blue, blue-green, brown, yellow and pale blue (aquamarine).

The mine uses a back hoe to uncover new material periodically. The mine area can be searched with shovel and screens. Use your screen to shift the red clay and uncover crystals. Beryl crystals grow in association with feldspar and mica.

Wear old clothing on your expedition. The red clay is especially hard on clothing and stains are often permanent.

VIRGINIA

Fairy Stones (Staurolite) - Fairy Stone State Park

REGION:
Southeast

ADDRESS:
Route 2, Box 723
Stuart, Virginia 24171
(540) 930-2424

DIRECTIONS:
Fairy Stone State Park is located in the foothills of the Blue Ridge Mountains in Patrick and Henry counties. Access to the park is via State Highway 57 from Bassett or U.S. Highway 58, or State Highways 8 and 57 from the Blue Ridge Parkway.

SEASON:
Best collecting is in the spring and summer.
The park is open year round.

HOURS:
Daylight

COST:
There is no fee for collecting Fairy Stones. The state park entrance fee is $2.00 per day to park. Camping is $15.00 per night.

WHAT TO BRING:
You will need a shovel, hand rake or trowel, pail or bucket to hold your fairy stones. A quarter-inch sifting screen may be helpful.

INFORMATION:
Fairy stones (staurolite crystals) can be found on the state park's property. These crystals form in various crosses and are very popular as religious necklaces. The access to the collecting area is left of the main park entrance on State Highway 57 at the first gas station on the left—"Haynes 57." The land at the left of the station is park land. A small parking lot is available. The State Parks Department requests that you only take a few samples for personal use.

The legend of the fairy stones is rather charming. It is said that local fairies lived and played in this glen. The fairies, upon hearing of the death of Christ, wept. Their tears crystallized into beautiful crosses. For years people have used these little crosses to protect against sickness, accidents and disaster.

This is the heart of Appalachia. The area has a strong tradition of crafts and music. The park is located in a very rural area.

NORTH CAROLINA

Gold Panning - Cotton Patch Gold Mine

REGION:
Southeast

ADDRESS:
41697 Gurley Road
New London, North Carolina 28127
(704) 463-5797

DIRECTIONS:
From Richfield, North Carolina, take U.S. Highway 52 to State Highway 740. Travel through New London and turn left on Gurley Road to the mine.

SEASON:
March 1 to December 15, Tuesday to Sunday

HOURS:
9:00 a.m. to 5:00 p.m.

COST:
Panning: $7.00 per person for five, two-gallon buckets of dirt
Sluicing: $12.00 for three, five-gallon buckets of dirt
Children under 12 — $3.50

WHAT TO BRING:
The mine will supply you with all the materials you need. You may bring your own standard mining tools. Motorized mining tools are not permitted.

INFORMATION:
     The Cotton Patch Gold Mine is a place where you can learn to pan and sluice for gold. The mine offers instruction to get you started. You may buy dirt by the bucket or by the front-end load. The costs range from $7.00 for a two-gallon bucket to $80.00 for a front-end load of material. This material is brought from a gold-producing area of the property. Panning troughs are provided to help you clean your concentrates. The stream has notched logs to ease the set-up of your sluice box.
     You will find picnic areas here and a general store that sells prospecting supplies, food and beverages. Camping with and without electric hook-ups is available. This is a fun, educational adventure for the entire family.
     On the last Sunday of October the Cotton Patch Gold Mine hosts a gold panning championship.

NORTH CAROLINA

Gold Panning - Reed Gold Mine

REGION:
Southeast

ADDRESS:
9621 Reed Mine Road
Stanfield, North Carolina 28163
(704) 786-8337

DIRECTIONS:
From Interstate 85 exit at Salisbury, North Carolina. Travel south on U.S. Highway 601 through the town of Concord to State Highway 200. Bear left onto State Highway 200 and drive 4 miles to Reed Mine Road. Turn left at the Reed Gold Mine sign into the mine.

SEASON:
April 1 to October 31
November 1 to March 31

HOURS:
Open April through October: Monday to Saturday, 9:00 a.m. to 5:00 p.m.,
Sunday, 1:00 p.m. to 5:00 p.m.
November to March: Closed Mondays, Tuesday to Saturday, 10:00 a.m. to 4:00 p.m.,
Sunday, 1:00 p.m. to 4:00 p.m.

COST:
Free

WHAT TO BRING:
Mining supplies are provided by the mine.

INFORMATION:
The Reed Gold Mine reported the first gold find in the United States. As the story goes, in 1799, Reed's son, Conrad, found a large yellow rock in the Little Meadow Creek while playing hooky from church. A silversmith in Concord was unable to identify the rock, but measured it's weight at 17 pounds. The Reeds used it as a door stop until a jeweler bought it in 1802, for $3.50, less than one-tenth of it's value. Later Reed discovered his mistake and "convinced" the jeweler to compensate him.

Mining later began by Reed and others and a 28-pound nugget was found. A total of $100,000 worth of gold was unearthed by 1824. The Reed Gold Mine has an underground tour, stamp mill for crushing rock, and a panning area. This area is open for panning only. The Reed Gold Mine is worth a visit for historical interest, don't expect to find a 20-pound nugget, because you are 100 years too late.

NORTH CAROLINA

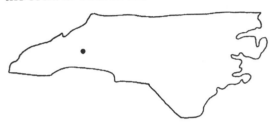

Gold Mining & Garnets - The Lucky Strike Gold Mine

REGION:
Southeast

ADDRESS:
The Lucky Strike Gold Mine
Route 5, Box 733
Marion, North Carolina 28752
(704) 738-4893

SEASON:
Open all year, weather permitting

HOURS:
8:00 a.m. to 6:00 p.m., daily

COST:
Panning or sluice box: $5.00 per day
Small dredge: $10.00 per day
Large dredge: $20.00 per day

DIRECTION:
From Marion, North Carolina, take Interstate 40 to U.S. Highway 221. Travel 5 miles south on U.S. Highway 221 and turn left onto Polly Sprout Road. Follow the road .3 mile to the mine entrance.

WHAT TO BRING:
Some supplies are available for rent including pans, dredges, high bankers and sluice boxes. You may use the troughes, poop tube and spiral wheel for concentrating your material for no charge. Bring standard gold mining equipment.

INFORMATION:
The Lucky Strike Gold Mine has all you need for a gold mining adventure. You will find a roofed area with several flumes. Here you can pan for some gemstones or get a gold panning lesson. This is also where the gold miners will gather in the evening to separate their concentrates.

Most miners who work this river will find some color. Many nuggets have been recovered here, as well as fine gold and flakes. The gold is often found in conjunction with the host quartz.

If you plan to camp, you can sluice or pan all day in the river for no additional charge. Lessons on dredging are given and you will learn all you need to know. You may also want to try high banking. The mine holds common digs throughout the year. This is an opportunity to join forces with others and have a weekend of gold mining. All the gold you find in the common digs is divided equally among the participating miners. Call the mine to find out more details.

Campsites with hookups are available right by the river. Restroom and shower facilities are also available. The Lucky Strike Gold Mine's "Miner Diner" has reasonably priced food for those too tuckered to cook. The owners are friendly and helpful.

NORTH CAROLINA

REGION:
Southeast

ADDRESS:
Route 5, Box 738
Marion, North Carolina 28752
(704) 738-3573

DIRECTIONS:
From Interstate 40 at Marion, North Carolina, take U.S. Highway 221 south to Polly Sprout Road. Look for the mine immediately on your left.

SEASON:
Open year round. Heated, indoor panning area available.

HOURS:
Daylight

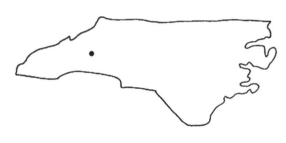

COST:
3-gallon gem buckets — $6.00
3-gallon gold buckets — $10.00
Sluice/pan — $6.00 per day
Dredging — $12.00 to $17.00
High banking — $17.00
Metal Detecting/dousing — $6.00

WHAT TO BRING:
Equipment is available to rent or bring your own gold mining equipment.

INFORMATION:
Opened in 1996, this nine-acre property is situated on a known gold-bearing stream beneath Vein Mountain. The mine offers a variety of recreational mining opportunities. You can sift through buckets for gems or pan out buckets of dirt. Or you can try your luck in the stream with a pan, sluice, high banker, or dredge.

Heather Grove is a family-oriented operation. The mine has a gift shop with supplies, food, and gifts for sale. RV and tent camping sites are available with or without hookups. There are also several new cabins with shower facilities for rent. One cabin is handicap accessible. There is a bath house for campers. Pets are permitted, but must be kept on a leash, so they do not disturb the owner's pet chickens and ducks.

NORTH CAROLINA

Blue Star Sapphires - Old Pressley Sapphire Mine

REGION:
Southeast

ADDRESS:
240 Pressley Mine Road
Canton, North Carolina 28716
(704) 648-6320

DIRECTION:
Take Exit 31 off Interstate 40 and go left to Canton. Drive past the paper factory and up the hill (away from the business district). Turn left onto North Hominy Road and follow the signs. Proceed left onto a dirt road. The Old Pressley Mine is the second mine on this dirt road.

SEASON:
Open all year round.
Flumes are open April 1 to October 31.

HOURS:
Open seven days a week, 9:00 a.m. to 6:00 p.m.

COST:
Adults — $5.00, group rates available
Children — $5.00
50¢ a bucket to process dirt.

WHAT TO BRING:
The mine supplies shovels, buckets, sifting screens and sluices. Bring your lunch or cooler. Chips and soda are available.

INFORMATION:
This is the home of the "Southern Star," the world's largest blue sapphire at 1,035 carats. The mine is set in a beautiful spot in Canton, North Carolina. The folks at the mine are friendly and helpful. They will answer all questions and offer tips on how to search. The sapphires that are found here are large in size. You will find blue star sapphires, but also gray, blue-gray, sky blue, corn silk blue and occasionally a pink sapphire.

Save all heavy stones that are covered with white feldspar and mica and have the experts at the mine check them for you. You may have missed a sapphire. A small rock shop is found in the office. Restrooms are available, but bring your own fresh water as the facility uses pond water.

NORTH CAROLINA

REGION:
Southeast

ADDRESS:
7091 Upper Burning Town Road
Franklin, North Carolina 28734
(704) 369-9742

DIRECTIONS:
Franklin, North Carolina is located approximately 25 miles south of Great Smoky Mountains National Park, and 60 miles southwest of Asheville, North Carolina. From Franklin, take State Highway 28 north toward the airport and look for the Mason sign on the left. Turn left onto State Road (SR) 1392/Upper Burning Town Road. It is 8.5 miles to the mine.

SEASON:
April 1 to October 31

HOURS:
Open daily from 9:00 a.m. to 5:00 p.m.

COST:
Adults — $10.00
Children ages 8 to 10 years — $7.00
Fee includes digging all day and all equipment

WHAT TO BRING:
All equipment is supplied, including: shovels, buckets, sorting screen boxes, even a film container to hold your loot. Bring your lunch. A picnic area is available. Some miners wear rubber gloves because the water in the sluice is cold.

INFORMATION:
Many of the mines in this area are seeded. This means they add stones to the dirt. The stones are from all over the world and are usually of poor quality. Most unseeded mines are a bit off the beaten track. This area has over 20 mines. Check with the Franklin Chamber of Commerce for details. Indigenous stones to Franklin County mines include sapphires and rubies.

The Mason Mine is not seeded and the digging is easy. You can have the stones cut in town at Ruby City and search through their shop at 130 E. Main Street in Franklin (704) 524-3967. The workers at the mine will explain the sifting of materials and how to spot the cylindrical sapphires. These stones are a clear, light pink when cut.

SOUTH CAROLINA

Amethyst Crystals - William's Property

REGION:
Southeast

ADDRESS:
Lorraine Williams
Route 2, Box 259
Donald's (Due West), South Carolina 29638
(864) 379-2148

DIRECTIONS:
The William's property is located on U.S. Highway 178. From Donald's, South Carolina, take State Highway 184, 4.1 miles to Due West, South Carolina. Turn left on State Highway 20 and go 1.2 miles, then take a left onto Ellis Road. Follow Ellis Road to the first brick house on the right.

SEASON:
April to October

HOURS:
8:00 a.m. to sundown

COST:
$6.00 dollars per day

WHAT TO BRING:
You will need a shovel, sifting screen with a quarter- to half-inch mesh, buckets and a closed container for your amethysts. No food is available so bring food and drinks.

INFORMATION:
This is a family-owned business, located in Abbeyville County, South Carolina. If you are planning a trip to the William's property to look for amethyst crystals, please call ahead two to three days in advance to make reservations. The digging is easy, so children can participate.

Some very nice amethyst crystals are found on the property. The amethyst is usually lilac or light purple in color. Occasionally a deep purple specimen is unearthed. It is possible to find small crystals lying on the surface in tailings piles, trails or open areas. Using a sifting screen can also prove productive. More ambitious miners look for quartz veins and use a crowbar and pick to access additional crystals.

Keep in mind that the most accessible spots have been picked over. To recover better specimens you will need to locate out of the way spots or overlooked areas.

GEORGIA

REGION:
Southeast

ADDRESS:
Route 8, Box 540
Hidden Valley Road
Dahlonega, Georgia 30533
(706) 864-7017

DIRECTIONS:
From Dahlonega, take U.S. Highway 52 east, 2 miles and turn left onto Rock House Road. Travel 1.6 miles and turn right onto Hidden Valley Road. Proceed .2 mile to the campsite.

SEASON:
March to December

HOURS:
Daylight

COST:
Pan/sluice — Free if you camp here, $2.00 if you don't
Dredging — $5.00 a day if you camp here, $10.00 if not

WHAT TO BRING:
Some supplies are available for rent. Bring standard gold mining equipment. Dredges are permitted.

INFORMATION:
The privately owned Hidden Valley Campground is located in the peaceful north Georgia hills in an area that was once Cherokee Indian territory. In the 1500s Spanish explorers traveled here in search for gold. They never found it, although it's here. Gold was first discovered in 1828 and is still being found today.

You can pan for gold or sluice or dredge in the two gold-bearing streams. Keep an eye out for gemstones such as garnets while you pan. The campground has 22 spaces for camping and RVs. Tent camping charges are $8.00 per night and RV sites with electric are $12.00 per night. Weekly and monthly rates are available. Facilities include restrooms, showers and nature trails. Campers may search for gold for no additional charge.

GEORGIA

REGION:
Southeast

ADDRESS:
2736 Morrison Moore Parkway
Dahlonega, Georgia 30533
(706) 864-6363

DIRECTIONS:
The Crisson Gold Mine is located 2.5 miles north of Dahlonega on U.S. Highway 19.
Look for the green and gold sign.

SEASON:
Open all year round

HOURS:
Summer: 10:00 a.m. to 6:00 p.m.
Winter: 10:00 a.m. to 5:00 p.m.

COST:
Panning: $2.00
By the bucket:
   2.5-gallon ore — $5.75   5-gallon ore — $8.50
   2-gallon gemstones — $3.50   5-gallon gemstones — $6.50

WHAT TO BRING:
The mine will supply you with gold pans and ore. For 50¢ you can buy a small bottle
to carry your gold away.

INFORMATION:
    The Crisson Gold Mine was established in 1847 during the Dahlonega gold rush
and is owned and operated by fourth generation gold miners. The mine has been
open to the public since 1970. This family-owned operation is now open to your
family for fun and adventure.
    The people at the mine will instruct you and help you pan or screen out your
material. The mine has an indoor facility for year-round treasure hunting. If you
don't want to pan for gold you can screen for gemstones. You may find rubies,
emeralds and numerous other stones.
    The Crisson Gold Mine has a gift shop open seven days a week. Gold, gold jew-
elry and gold nuggets can be purchased. Some gold mining equipment, used commercially, is on display.

GEORGIA

*Gold Panning -
Pine Mountain Gold Mine
& Theme Park*

REGION:
Southeast

ADDRESS:
1881 Stockmar Road
Villa Rica, Georgia 30180
(770) 456-0921

DIRECTIONS:
Pine Mountain Gold Mine and Theme Park is located off U.S. Highway 20 between
Douglasville and Tallapoosa in the town of Villa Rica.

SEASON:
Open all year round.

HOURS:
Daylight

COST:
Panning and prospecting: $5.00 per day
Camping (primitive): $5.00 per night

WHAT TO BRING:
Some supplies are available for rent. Bring standard gold mining equipment. Dredges
are permitted.

INFORMATION:
Located in Georgia's Golden Mountains, near Villa Rica and Tallapoosa, Pine
Mountain was a working mine until it became unprofitable in the 1920s.

Pine Mountain Gold Mine and Theme Park opened in 1993, offering visitors the
opportunity to do most types of gold mining including gold panning, sluicing, high
banking and dredging at a reasonable price. The park has primitive camping sites
available. Tours of the mine are available at no charge to overnight campers. There is
a gold museum which houses mining tools and equipment used during the original
mine operation.

You are allowed to look for gold or gemstones and keep what you find. If you find
any relics from the Georgia gold rush in the 1820s, such as picks or shovels, you are
asked to donate them to the museum.

FLORIDA

1715 Spanish Treasure - Vero Beaches

REGION:
Southeast

ADDRESS:
Highway A1A
Sebastian Inlet, Florida
(407) 567-3491, Vero Chamber
of Commerce

DIRECTIONS:
All beach sites are off State Highway A1A, from Sebastian Inlet to Fort Pierce Inlet. Some beach accesses are: Wabasso Beach, Seagrape Beach, and Turtle Trail Beach.

SEASON:
All seasons. After winter storms are the most productive times for finding treasure.

HOURS:
See public beach signs for hours. Beaches are generally open from 7:00 a.m. to dusk.

COST:
Beach access is free.
The museum is $1.00.

WHAT TO BRING:
A good metal detector with a discriminator to exclude false signals from mineralized sand is essential. Also needed are a sand scoop and pouch to carry finds and remove trash. The shipwreck survivors were driven insane by mosquitoes, so bring bug spray and a hat.

INFORMATION:
   On July 24, 1715, 11 Spanish Galleons were struck by a hurricane. Since that time gold and silver coins called *escudos* and *reals* have been found on these beaches. Lucky rockhounds have even found green emeralds from these ships. The beaches are good places for modern coins and shells. Please follow local regulations and stay on the walkovers to the beaches. Stay off the dunes, watch out for turtle nests and carry out your trash.
   Use of a good metal detector is strongly recommended. Many ships, including metal ones, have broken apart on these beaches. So a good discriminator on your detector in a must. Coins are difficult, but not impossible to find. Using a metal detector in the water is forbidden by Admiralty Claims. Stay off private property. Stop and see the McLarty Museum 1.9 miles north of Sebastian Inlet (10:00 a.m. to 4:45 p.m.) when you need a break.

FLORIDA

Fossilized Shark's Teeth - Venice Public Beaches

REGION:
Southeast

ADDRESS:
Chamber of Commerce
257 North Tamiami Trail
Venice, Florida 34285
(941) 488-2236

DIRECTIONS:
Take Interstate 75 or U.S. Highway 41 to Venice, Florida. Take Venice Avenue to the Venice Public Beach.

SEASON:
Open all year round

HOURS:
Daylight

COST:
Free

WHAT TO BRING:
You can find teeth without equipment. Your success rate will be better if you have a metal tooth scooper with a long handle, home-made screens or even pasta strainers. Bring a closed container to keep your shark's teeth. Swimsuit pockets tend to give back your treasures to the sea, and are not recommended.

INFORMATION:
All of Venice's public beaches are good places to look for shark teeth. Try Venice Beach, Venice Fishing Pier and Caspersen State Park. Many teeth are found washed up on the beach or in ankle-deep water in the surf. Some enterprising individuals snorkel or scuba dive for teeth and other fossils. Look for black sand and small rocks, these are fossil deposits. People on the beach are friendly and willing to share hunting techniques with you. They will also show you their haul if asked.

Teeth range in size from a quarter inch to six inches. You will find more of the former and fewer of the latter. Bring sandals or sneakers. The black sand gets HOT and you'll never make it back to your car without them. Keep your eyes open for fossilized bones which are black with little holes in them where blood vessels once were. Stop by the Sea Pleasure and Treasures Gift Shop in Venice and see the amazing teeth on display and for sale.

FLORIDA

Sea Shell Hunting - Sanibel & Captiva Islands

REGION:
Southeast

ADDRESS:
Sanibel Chamber of Commerce
1159 Causeway Road
Sanibel, Florida 33957
(941) 472-3232

DIRECTIONS:
Sanibel Island is located southwest of Fort Meyers. Follow signs to the Sanibel Causeway and beaches.

SEASON:
Open all year round

HOURS:
Daylight or night, although the best finds occur at the changing of the tides.

COST:
None

WHAT TO BRING:
You may want to bring a pail, shell identification book, flashlight for night hunting and a really loud tropical shirt.

INFORMATION:
   Sanibel and Captiva Islands are renowned as the best shell hunting beaches in the world and Turner Beach is known for the best collecting. Keep in mind there are so many great shells to be found here, that you should not take live shells. This will destroy future populations, so you should return shellfish that still reside in the shell you may pick up.
   The best time to search is early in the morning when the tide is going out. Bring a flashlight for searching at night as well. Early risers are rewarded by having the days first pick of scattered shells.
   Most of Florida's barrier islands have some fine shells, but Sanibel and Captiva are unique. Barrier islands lie parallel to the coast, but Sanibell is shaped like a fish hook. The portion of beach that sticks out into the gulf acts to catch shells.
   The community here has done a excellent job of controlling development. The building codes are very strict. For you, this means that there are no highrises spoiling the view. From the beach, the hotels and condos are all at tree level and set back, to be unobtrusive. The shops and stores are also low and recessed with small, non-illuminated signs, creating a very picturesque spot for a vacation.

MICHIGAN

REGION:
Midwest

ADDRESS:
2475 M-119
Petoskey, Michigan 49712
(616) 347-2311

SEASON:
April 1 to October 31

HOURS:
Park headquarters are open 9:00 a.m. to 5:00 p.m.

COST:
Nominal admission charged by the car.
Camping is $15.00 per night.

WHAT TO BRING:
Bring a small pail to hold your stones.

DIRECTIONS:
Take Interstate 75 north to Indian River. Go west on State Highway 68 to Alanson. At Alanson take U.S. Highway 31 southeast to State Highway 119 north. The park is 4 miles from this junction and located on Lake Michigan.

INFORMATION:
   Petoskey became Michigan's state stone in 1965. Petoskey stone's scientific name is hexagonaria percarinata. This stone was once a living colony of coral on the ocean floor. It is now fossilized into a white, brown or gray stone. The striations and swirling circular pattern is what remains of the coral animal. When wet or polished the stone shows tiny rings, resembling a honeycomb; dry it is silvery with no markings.

   This fossilized coral colony weathered out of limestone and was widely distributed by glacial action. Petoskey stones are common in Michigan along the Northern and Southern Peninsulas. In the state park they are rounded and polished by wave action and deposited on the beach.

   This stone is used in jewelry, decorative items, sculpture and, of course, as paper weights. It is beautiful and relatively easy to carve. Each stone is unique and no two are alike.

   The park is located on 305 acres, along Little Traverse Bay. They have a swimming area on the lakeshore. Facilities include a beach house, playground, picnic area and camping facilities. Boating and hiking are popular pastimes in this lovely park. Nearby, is the historic Gaslight Shopping District, which is worth a trip if you have the time.

MICHIGAN

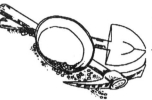

Copper -
Delaware Copper Mine

REGION:
Midwest

ADDRESS:
Box 148
U.S. 41
Kearsarge, Michigan 49942
(906) 289-4688

SEASON:
May to October

HOURS:
10:00 a.m. to 5:00 p.m., daily
Open until 6:00 p.m. — June, July, August

COST:
Adults — $6.00
Children 6 to 12 years — $3.50
Children under 6 years — free

WHAT TO BRING:
Bring standard mining tools, your own food and
plenty to drink. There is a picnic area here.

DIRECTIONS:
The Delaware Copper Mine is located on
the Keeweenaw Peninsula and Lake
Superior, south of Isle Royal National
Park. From Hancock, Michigan, take U.S.
Highway 41 north 43 miles to Copper
Harbor. Follow the signs.

INFORMATION:
   One of the oldest mines in the area, the Delaware Copper Mine began operations
in 1847 and produced over eight million pounds of copper from its five shafts. The
mine closed in 1887, but is now open for tours. You will travel to the first level at
110 feet below the ground and see pure veins of copper in the walls of the mine. You
will learn of the area's mine history and operations.
   Tours leave every 20 minutes and take 45 minutes. The tour includes a tram ride,
elevator descent and easy walking. Comfortable footwear and jackets are recommended by the mine. The temperature underground is a constant 45 degrees.
   Also found here is a gift shop, mining museum, petting zoo and remains of
mining buildings. Visitors are permitted to search for souvenirs from the mine's half-
mile-long tailings pile of rock, dirt and copper. Pieces of copper range from thumbnail
sized to half-a-pound. No metal detectors are permitted.

INDIANA

Fossils -
Interstate 64 Road Cut

REGION:
Midwest

ADDRESS:
Interstate 64
Exit 86
Crawford County, Indiana
No phone

DIRECTIONS:
Take I-64 to Sulphur, Indiana in Crawford County. Exit at Exit 86. The road cut is directly off the exit.

SEASON:
Open all year round

HOURS:
Daylight

COST:
Free

WHAT TO BRING:
Bring standard mining tools, your own food and plenty to drink. Also include a collecting bucket, small rock hammer, prying tools or hand garden tools and a small broom or brush.

INFORMATION:
This site is a bit different. It is not a private mine or public park. It is a road cut. Unearthed by the construction of Interstate 64, this area is rich in fossils. It has become a very popular site for local rock hunters. Since it is located along the exits of Interstate 64, there is no organization or phone number listed above to provide additional information. But if your travels take you along Interstate 64 you may want to take Exit 86 to have a look around.

This area contains many types of fossils including crinoids, fish remains, horn coral, shark's teeth, snails and brachiopods. Material is found in shale and limestone deposits. The best areas to find fossils are on the northwest and northeast corners of the exit. There is plenty of parking. Please respect the area and other collectors. Collecting is for personal use only. Search at your own risk.

MISSOURI

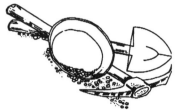

*Geode Mine -
Sheffler's Rock Shop*

REGION:
Midwest

ADDRESS:
R.R. 1, Box 172
Alexandria, Missouri 63430
(816) 754-6443

DIRECTIONS:
The Sheffler's Rock Shop and Geode Mine is located on U.S. Highway 61 between
Canton, Missouri, and Keokuk, Iowa.

SEASON:
April 1 to December 1, weather permitting

HOURS:
Open seven days a week, 9:00 a.m. to 5:00 p.m.

COST:
$10.00 per person per day

WHAT TO BRING:
Bring standard mining tools, your own food and plenty to drink.

INFORMATION:
Sheffler's Rock Shop and Geode Mine is located in northeast Missouri, close to
the Illinois and Iowa borders. The geode mine is a safe and easy way for the whole
family to have a rockhounding adventure. Stop at the rock shop first to arrange to
dig and to see the display of opened geodes from the mine. The shop has minerals
for sale including rough cut rock, agates, slabs, supplies and jewelry mountings.

Geodes are bubbles of rocks that resemble stone snowballs. They are formed by
volcanic action. Although the exterior is quite plain, the interior can be spectacular.
They are ocassionally hollow and filled with crystals. The weight of the geode may
indicate to you if it is hollow. The trick, of course, is getting into them. You will need
a rock saw or access to one to see if you have a unique specimen.

The mine allows you 50 pounds of material for each admission ticket. If you
collect over 50 pounds of geodes, you pay 50¢ per pound. Bring your own lunch and
have a great day looking for geodes.

ARKANSAS

Quartz Crystals -
Robins Mining
Company

REGION:
Midwest

ADDRESS:
P.O. Box 236
Mount Ida, Arkansas 71957
(501) 867-2530

DIRECTIONS:
The Robins Mining Company is located at the junction of U.S. Highway 270 and
State Highway 27 south. As of the writing of this book there is an Exxon Gas Station
at this junction in Mount Ida, Arkansas.

SEASON:
Open all year

HOURS:
9:00 a.m. to 5:00 p.m.,
Monday through Friday

COST:
$10.00 per day

WHAT TO BRING:
Bring standard mining tools, your own food and plenty to drink.

INFORMATION:
    The Robins Mining Company is one of the oldest and most reliable crystal mining
operations in Arkansas. This is a family-owned business passed from father to son.
Specimens found here are the only ones in the area that produce blue and smoky
phantom crystals. Clear quartz crystals are also found at the mine.
    Quartz is found in the open crystal pockets that form in the sandstone, shale and
other rocks in the Ouachita Mountains of Arkansas. The crystals are hexagonal in
structure and have the unique ability to amplify, transform and transfer energy. They
are used in electronics, radios and watches. The crystals are believed to have healing
properties by many in the metaphysical field and are often used during meditation.
    The Robins Mining Company has a shop called the Crystal House where they sell
and ship crystals. If you cannot visit the mine, the Robins family can supply you
with a price list of crystals, cluster crystals, single points, smoky enhanced clusters,
amethysts, spheres and tumbled stones.

ARKANSAS

*Quartz Crystals -
The Starfire Mine*

REGION:
Midwest

ADDRESS:
H.C. 63
P.O. Box 306
Mount Ida, Arkansas 71957
(501) 867-2431

DIRECTIONS:
The Starfire Mine is located 11 miles east of Mount Ida on U.S. Highway 270. As of the writing of this book the mine is next to the Colonial Motel.

SEASON:
Open year round

HOURS:
6:30 a.m. until dark

COST:
$20.00 per person

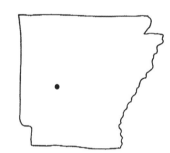

WHAT TO BRING:
Bring standard mining tools, your own food and plenty to drink.

INFORMATION:
    The Starfire Mine is recommended for more experienced miners, due to the amount of digging that must be done. This mine is not cleared by heavy equipment, so digging is harder and more strenuous.

    Some good finds have come out of the Starfire Mine. If you have experience and your own tools, it is worth the stop. Starfire Mine also sells quartz crystals wholesale and retail to the public.

    To discover more about this area you may want to write ahead of time for information from the Mount Ida Area Chamber of Commerce at P.O. Box 6, Mount Ida, Arkansas 71957. They can be reached by phone at (501) 867-2723. The Chamber of Commerce sponsors an annual Quartz, Quiltz and Craftz Festival in October which you may want to attend if you are in the area. A crystal quartz dig is part of the festivities.

ARKANSAS

Quartz Crystals - Wegner Crystal Mines & Ranch

REGION:
Midwest

ADDRESS:
P.O. Box 205
Mount Ida, Arkansas 71957
(501) 867-2309

DIRECTIONS:
The Wegner Crystal Mines are located 6 miles south of Mount Ida, off State Highway 27 on Owley Road. Follow the signs on Owley Road to the mine.

SEASON:
Open all year, seven days a week, weather and holidays permitting

HOURS:
8:00 a.m. to 5:00 p.m.

COST:
Phantom Mine: $20.00
Crystal Forest Mine: $15.00
Old Mountain Top: $8.00
Salted Mine (for children and seniors): $6.00
Admission to all the mines is half-price for children under 12.

WHAT TO BRING:
Bring standard mining tools, your own food and plenty to drink.

INFORMATION:
   The Wegner Crystal Mines have something for everyone. This is an extensive operation which is actually four separate mines. The Phantom Mine is the most productive and popular mine and has produced world-famous phantom crystals. The Crystal Forest Mine is located on 40 acres and produces clear, gem-quality crystals. Old Mountain Top has breathtaking views and involves a strenuous climb. The mine recommends that only experienced hikers try this mine; children will have trouble making the trip. The Salted Mine is for children and seniors looking for guaranteed success. It is readily accessible and is located adjacent to the campground.
   They have a tourist center which will orient you to the options available. At the center you will find a large collection of quartz crystals, minerals and fossils for sale. Snacks, sandwiches and beverages are also sold here. The mine has camping facilities with showers, restrooms, a fishing area and swimming. There is also a specimen museum and a 10,000-square-foot wholesale barn where specimens are for sale.

ARKANSAS

*Quartz Crystals -
Crystal Pyramid Mine*

REGION:
Midwest

ADDRESS:
H.C. 63
P.O. Box 136A
Mount Ida, Arkansas 71957
(501) 867-2568

DIRECTIONS:
The Crystal Pyramid Mine is located 4 miles east of Mount Ida, Arkansas on U.S. Highway 270.

SEASON:
Open all year

HOURS:
9:00 a.m. to 5:00 p.m.

COST:
$20.00 worth of rocks at the shop gives you a free pass to mine all day or it is $10.00 per person per day to mine

WHAT TO BRING:
Bring standard mining tools, your own food and plenty to drink.

INFORMATION:
  Ask for permission before you dig. This is a small operation. The area is being cleared by machinery at this time, making crystals easier to find. This area is known to produce crystals of excellent quality. This mine is not recommended for inexperienced miners or children. You will need to bring your own tools and expect a hard day of mining to see if you can find the big one.

  If you don't have any luck you may want to stop at the Crystal Pyramid Rock Shop on your way out. The shop sells a wide variety of rocks and minerals as do several other rock shops in the area.

  To discover more about this area you may want to check with the Mount Ida Area Chamber of Commerce at P.O. Box 6, Mount Ida, Arkansas 71957, (501) 867-2723. The Chamber of Commerce sponsors an annual Quartz, Quiltz and Craftz Festival in October which includes a crystal quartz dig. There is no admission charge for the festival.

ARKANSAS

Quartz Crystals - Fiddler's Ridge Rock Shop & Crystal Mine

REGION:
Midwest

ADDRESS:
H.C. 63
Box 211-J
Mount Ida, Arkansas 71957
(501) 867-2127

DIRECTIONS:
The Fiddler's Ridge Rock Shop and Mine is located 7 miles east of Mount Ida, Arkansas on U.S. Highway 270. The Crystal Mine is located approximately 5 miles from the rock shop.

SEASON:
Year round

HOURS:
The mine is open daylight hours.
The rock shop is open 9:00 a.m. to 5:00 p.m.

COST:
Adults — $10.00 per day
Children under 12 — $5.00

WHAT TO BRING:
Bring standard mining tools, your own food and plenty to drink.

INFORMATION:
Stop at the Fiddler's Ridge Rock Shop to get a permit to mine. We suggest you get a permit the day before, so you can set out early on your adventure. It is cool in the morning, but gets hot in the afternoon. The mine is open until dark and produces some fine crystals.

The Fiddler's Ridge Rock Shop has a large supply of mineral specimens, polished stones and unfinished stones for the rock hobbyist. Jewelry and speciality gift items are available with the native Mount Ida crystals.

Camping is available two miles from the shop at Lake Ouachita. Restaurants and motels are also nearby.

ARKANSAS

*Quartz Crystals -
Ocus Stanley & Son*

REGION:
Midwest

ADDRESS:
P.O. Box 163
Mount Ida, Arkansas 71957
(501) 867-3556, (501) 867-3719 after 5:00 p.m.

DIRECTIONS:
Ocus Stanley & Son is located on Pine Street off U.S. Highway 270, east of Mount Ida.

SEASON:
Open daily, year round

HOURS:
8:30 a.m. to 5:00 p.m.

COST:
Donations accepted

WHAT TO BRING:
Bring standard mining tools, your own food and plenty to drink. The mine owners recommend a hammer, screwdriver or tire iron. Anything you can scratch around with in the dirt will be fine. The owners kindly remind us that red clay stains are difficult to get out of clothing, so wear old clothes to the digging site.

INFORMATION:
The Fisher and Stanley families have mined this area through five generations. During World War II the fine gem-quality crystals were used for oscillators (radio chips). The family rock shop has been in business since the 1940s and still occupies the same location. Over 300 types of minerals are for sale at the shop. The crystal clusters from the mine are particularly decorative. The family's private collection has become a small museum which is available for viewing upon request.

The Ocus Stanley & Son Mine is located ten miles from the shop. You can drive all the way up Fisher Mountain to the digging site. There are lovely mountain views from the mine area. Enjoy the scenery while you try your luck.

You will need to clean the crystals that you find at the mine in a mild acid to remove dirt and rust stains. Use one pound of oxalic acid and two-and-a-half gallons of water. Use any container, but aluminum, and heat the water until all the acid is dissolved. Place the crystals in the solution and cover. Allow the crystals to soak for four or five days. The solution will be good for up to three uses.

ARKANSAS

Diamonds -
Crater of Diamonds
State Park

REGION:
Midwest

ADDRESS:
Route 1, Box 364
Murfreesboro, Arkansas 71958
(501) 285-3113

SEASON:
Open all year round

HOURS:
8:00 a.m. to 5:00 p.m.

COST:
Adults — $4.00
Children — $1.50

DIRECTIONS:
The park is situated midway between Hot Springs and Texarkana, Arkansas. From Texarkana take Interstate 30 north and exit at Hope (Exit 30). Take State Highway 4 northwest to Nashville. Then take State Highway 27 northwest towards Murfreesboro. At Murfreesboro take State Highway 301 southeast to the park.

WHAT TO BRING:
Bring equipment for diamond mining. Also include a large washtub, sprayer bottle, rubber boots, and screens with varying size mesh (quarter inch and one-eighth inch). A plastic container with a lid is suggested for holding your finds. Equipment may also be rented from the park with a deposit and I.D.

INFORMATION:
In this rare 36-acre field, diamonds of various colors and sizes can be found in their natural matrix. They are not easy to find, but an average of over 600 diamonds are found here each year. Over 70,000 have been found so far. The largest recovered was the 40.23-carat diamond called the Uncle Sam. The 15.33-carat diamond, Star of Arkansas, worn by Mrs. Clinton at her husband's inauguration, was also found here.

Diamonds can be located by surface inspection, surface scratching, sifting, digging and washing. Dirt is turned monthly to expose new soil. You are looking for well-rounded crystals usually smaller than a pea. Diamonds are naturally coated with oil and resist mud or dirt. Look for clean crystals. The most common colors are white, brown and yellow. Bring anything you think might be a diamond to the visitor center for verification and weighing. Anything you find, you keep.

Diamonds are the chief attraction here, but don't overlook the other gems and minerals such as amethyst, agate, jasper, quartz, calcite and barite.

The visitor center offers orientation programs on nature, geology, mining methods and history. The park has 60 campsites with water and electrical hookups. There is a bathhouse, restrooms, exhibits and gift shop within the park. Restaurants and motels are nearby.

ARKANSAS

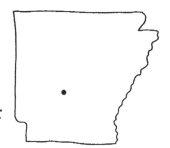

Quartz Crystals - Coleman's Quartz Mine

REGION:
Midwest

ADDRESS:
P.O. Box 8219
Hot Springs, Arkansas 71909
(501) 984-5396 or (501) 624-7280

DIRECTIONS:
From Hot Springs take State Highway 7 northwest for 14 miles to the mine.

SEASON:
Open year round

HOURS:
8:00 a.m. to 5:00 p.m.,
8:00 a.m. to 6:00 p.m. during the summer

COST:
Adults — $20.00
Children 7 to 16 — $5.00
Children 6 and under — Free

WHAT TO BRING:
Bring standard mining tools, your own food and plenty to drink. Tools are also available for rent from the mine.

INFORMATION:
This area has been mined commercially for many years. The ground at the mine is an open pit, turned over by a bulldozer. Over 40 acres of tailings are available. Tailings piles are piles of stone broken up and searched by the mine. Many good crystals are overlooked. Crystals are guaranteed to be found by experienced rockhounds or "pebble pups." The mine provides crystal washing stations in the digging area.

The mine has a gift shop and a wholesale showroom. The mine is located close to Hot Springs National Park. After visiting the park, you might want to visit Coleman's gift shop and browse their large selection of quartz, amethyst, agate and other minerals.

The Crystal Ridge RV Park is located on the grounds of the mining company and has sites for RVs and tent campers. Twenty-six sites include water and electricity. Modern restrooms, dump stations and laundry are available to guests.

OKLAHOMA

Selenite Crystals - Salt Plains National Wildlife Refuge

REGION:
Midwest

ADDRESS:
Salt Plains National Wildlife Refuge
Jet, Oklahoma 73749
(405) 626-4794

DIRECTIONS:
From Cherokee, Oklahoma, take U.S. Highway 64 south 3 miles. Then travel 6 miles east on a paved country road following the signs to Selenite Crystal Collecting Area.

SEASON:
April 1 to October 15

HOURS:
Daylight

COST:
Free

WHAT TO BRING:
Take along small garden tools, a shovel, a container to hold your crystals, and your own food and water. A change of clothes, socks and shoes are recommended as you are likely to get wet. Sunscreen is also recommended.

INFORMATION:
Selenite crystals are crystallized gypsum, brownish in color and somewhat translucent. The crystals are found just below the the thin layer of salt covering the muddy soil.

Dig carefully into the mud, using the water that seeps into the hole. Splash the water onto the sides of the hole to expose the crystals in the hole wall. The crystals found here range from single selenite crystals a few inches long to clusters weighing several pounds. Single, twin and clusters of crystals are are also found. Ten pounds of crystals per day are permitted to be removed for personal use.

Be sure to wear old clothes as the salt and mud will stain. A cushion or pad to kneel upon is recommended. Crystals newly exposed from the mud are fragile and you should place them in a carton or box to dry.

No camping is permitted. Camping is, however, available on the east side of the lake in the Great Salt Plains Dam and State Park. The nearby town of Cherokee has several restaurants and two motels to choose from.

OKLAHOMA

Petrified Wood & Algae, Agates - Roberts Ranch

REGION:
Midwest

ADDRESS:
Roberts Ranch
H.C.R. 1, Box #2
Kenton, Oklahoma 73946
(405) 261-7410

DIRECTIONS:
From Kenton, Oklahoma, proceed east about 2 miles on State Highway 325. Turn north onto the ranch road and drive 2.3 miles, bearing left at all forks to the Roberts' home.

SEASON:
Open all year round,
Monday through Saturday

HOURS:
8:00 a.m. to 5:00 p.m.

COST:
25¢ per pound for petrified wood, rose agate and jasper

WHAT TO BRING:
You may find agates without tools. A shovel, pick, gloves and a bucket will be helpful.

INFORMATION:
   Roberts Ranch is located in the Black Mesa Canyon area. Their property is actually located on one of the mesas. You can search all day along the Cimarron River banks and up the hills on each side. Many specimens can be found without digging. Digging is permitted along the river, but be sure to fill in your holes. The river may be the best place to search for petrified algae, while the surrounding hills are better areas to find petrified wood. Rattlesnakes have been know to visit this area.
   Some samples are quite large, as you can see from the petrified logs and stumps displayed in the Roberts' yard. Most prevalent is rose agate and petrified wood, although all types of agates are found here. Most of the petrified wood found is brown and black. Cycads, a nodular rock, are also occasionally found, although they are rare. Camping is permitted on their property, although there are no facilities. Camping is also available at nearby Black Mesa State Park.

TEXAS

Topaz -
Garner Seaquist Ranch

REGION:
Midwest

ADDRESS:
P.O. Box 35
Mason, Texas 76856
(512) 352-6415

DIRECTIONS:
Pick up keys and pay fees at the Nu-Way Grocery on the northwest corner of the square in Mason. To get to the mine take U.S. Highway 87 north. From the Mason Courthouse it is 1.25 miles to a blinking yellow light. Turn left at the light onto U.S. Highway 377/State Highway 29. Continue 1.4 miles to the fork in the road with a roadside park in the middle. Keep right (toward Menard) another .5 mile.

SEASON:
Open all year round, except October through December, during hunting season.

HOURS:
Daylight

COST:
$10.00 per person per day
$5.00 for camping in primitive sites

WHAT TO BRING:
You will need a pick and shovel, spray bottle of water, container with a lid, and a quarter-inch wire sifting screen.

INFORMATION:
Mason County is known for its topaz, which can be found in a range of colors including clear brown, yellow and sky blue. Searching for topaz is ideal after a few days of rain. Rain softens the ground and shows off the topaz. The mine will let you hunt all day and keep all the stones you find. The terrain is rocky with little shade.

No reservations are needed. Pay fees and pick up the keys at the Nu-Way Grocery on the northwest corner of the square in Mason. The Loefflers also have the keys to the Garner Seaquist Ranch. The Loefflers live in the white house on the right side of the road in Grit, Texas, near this mine and the Wayne Hofmann Ranch.

TEXAS

Topaz -
Wayne Hofmann Ranch

REGION:
Southwest

ADDRESS:
Wesley Loefflers
Route 8C 85, Box 6
Mason, Texas 76856
(915) 347-6415

DIRECTIONS:
Take U.S. Highway 87 north from Mason Courthouse 1.25 miles to a blinking yellow light. Turn left at the light onto U.S. Highway 377/State Highway 29. Continue 1.4 miles to the fork in the road with a roadside park in the middle. Keep right (toward Menard) another .5 mile. The Loefflers live in the white house on the right side of the road in Grit, Texas.

SEASON:
Open all year round, except October through December, during hunting season.

HOURS:
Daylight

COST:
Adults — $10.00 per person per day
Children ages six to ten — $5.00
Children under six years — Free

WHAT TO BRING:
Bring standard mining equipment, a spray bottle of water, a container with a lid, and a quarter-inch wire sifting screen.

INFORMATION:
Mason County is known for its topaz in colors ranging from clear brown to yellow to sky blue. Searching for topaz is ideal after a few days of rain. Rain softens the ground and shows off the topaz. The mine will let you hunt all day and keep all the stones you find. The terrain is rocky with little shade.

The town of Mason has many shops that sell topaz and topaz jewelry as well as guided topaz tours. Other area attractions include the Eckert James River Bat Cave with a large colony of Mexican free-tailed bats.

SOUTH DAKOTA

Gold Panning - Big Thunder Gold Mine

REGION:
Midwest

ADDRESS:
P.O. Box 459
Keystone, South Dakota 57751
(605) 666-4847 or (800) 843-1300, ext.774

DIRECTIONS:
Turn left at the stoplight in Keystone, South Dakota. The Big Thunder Gold Mine is located just around the next corner about three blocks away.

SEASON:
May 1 to October 1
Off season by reservation

HOURS:
8:00 a.m. to 8:00 p.m.

COST:
Tour Admissions:
  Big Miners — $5.50
  Little Miners — $3.50
  Under 6 years — Free

Gold Panning — $5.50 per pan
There is a $2.00 discount to tour and pan.

WHAT TO BRING:
All supplies are provided by the mine.

INFORMATION:
    The Big Thunder Gold Mine is in the Black Hills of South Dakota. The mine was claimed by two German immigrants in 1882. These men tunneled 138-feet into the mountain in their search for gold.

    Visitors to the Big Thunder Gold Mine will view a short film on the area's geology and history. The film is followed by a mining tour along a 130-foot tunnel which is well lit and spacious. You will tour this underground mine with some knowledgeable and friendly people. At the tour's end you will be allowed to dig your own genuine gold ore. For an additonal fee you can pan for gold in the stream at the mine.

    Wear a light jacket and comfortable shoes on the mine tour. The temperature underground is a constant 50 degrees.

SOUTH DAKOTA

Gold Panning - Wade's Gold Mill

REGION:
Midwest

ADDRESS:
Box 312
Hill City, South Dakota 57745
(605) 574-2680 or 2279

DIRECTIONS:
Take U.S. Highway 385 and U.S. Highway 16 to Hill City, South Dakota. In Hill City turn up the hill on Deerfield Road by the convenience store and the Super 8 Motel. Go .75 mile on the blacktop to the mine.

SEASON:
Memorial Day to Labor Day

HOURS:
Two-hour tours starting at 9:30 a.m. and 1:30 p.m.

COST:
Mill and Museum Tour:
Adults — $5.00
Children — $2.50
Gold Panning: $5.00 - $10.00

WHAT TO BRING:
Wade's Gold Mill will supply you with all the equipment you need.

INFORMATION:
Wade's Gold Mill is an educational experience for the whole family. You will learn local mining history and see the working and processing of gold.

The museum tour gives visitors a good look at what mining was like during the South Dakota gold rush of 1874. Gold mining and mill processing equipment has been gathered and reconstructed into a working operation. There is a mining photo gallery of old time miners and area mill operations. This is a living history museum. The mill tour is a tour of a placer mill that shows how a mill operates.

A short panning lesson is offered which lasts about ten minutes. The long panning lesson goes into more detail and lasts about an hour. Both teach the basics of panning for gold.

COLORADO

Petrified Wood, Coprolite, Rose Agate - Layton Ranch

REGION:
Southwest

ADDRESS:
Layton Ranch
Colorado Route
Kenton, Oklahoma 73946
(719) 461-7457

DIRECTIONS:
Layton's Ranch is 4 miles from the tri-state marker of New Mexico, Oklahoma and Colorado. From New Mexico take State Highway 406 to State Highway 456. This becomes State Highway 325 at the Oklahoma border. Travel to Kenton, Oklahoma. Five-tenths of a mile outside of Kenton, you will see Ranch Road on the left. Take it 11.2 miles out of Oklahoma to Colorado. Ranch Road dead ends onto Country Road 8. Go right (east) on Country Road 8 and proceed 2.3 miles to Road B. Turn left onto Road B and proceed 400 yards to the Layton's ranch.

SEASON:
Open all year round

HOURS:
Daylight

COST:
Very reasonable prices. Some material is free. Petrified wood is 10¢ a pound. Coprolite and petrified dinosaur bone are $10.00 to $20.00 per pound.

WHAT TO BRING:
You can search without tools by the river or bring your own digging tools.

INFORMATION:
　　The Layton Ranch has a bit of everything. Most prevalent is the petrified wood and rose agate. There is also petrified algae, coprolite (petrified dinosaur droppings), and petrified dinosaur bones. Specimens occur in a wide variety of colors including brown, black, green, red, yellow and blue. Mr. Layton will give you directions on where you may search. He asks that you call ahead so he will know to expect you.
　　The search area is not cleared of vegetation. You will need to break through the brush to get to the rocks. Easier searching can be had by the river. There are no facilities, food or beverage here. Bring what you need with you. You can camp at Black Mesa State Park, 27 miles south in Oklahoma, or Two Buttes Park, 30 miles north.

COLORADO

Gold Panning - Bachelor - Syracuse Mine Tour

REGION:
Southwest

ADDRESS:
P.O. Box 380 W.
Ouray, Colorado 81427
(970) 325-4500

DIRECTIONS:
The Bachelor - Syracuse Mine is located in Ouray, Colorado. Take Country Road 14 to Dexter Creek Road. Follow the signs to the mine.

SEASON:
May 20 to September 15 (closed July 4th)

HOURS:
10:00 a.m. to 5:00 p.m. (May)
9:00 a.m. to 6:00 p.m. (June - August)

COST:
Tours:
Adults — $8.95
Children under 11 years — $4.95
Gold panning: $4.95

WHAT TO BRING:
The mine will supply you with the equipment you need to pan for gold and give you a small bottle to hold your finds. This mine has great barbecue so there is no need to pack food.

INFORMATION:
Ouray is a town with a rich mining history. It is very scenic and worth the drive through the Rocky Mountains. The Bachelor Mine is a clean, well-maintained silver and gold mine. Silver was discovered here in 1884 by three bachelors, thus the name. The mine has produced 15 million ounces of silver and a quarter million ounces of gold as well as lead, zinc and copper.

The tour is conducted by trained guides who can answer all your mining questions and relate their local history. A mine train (trammer) is boarded to advance into the mine. You will visit the work areas and see how explosives are used. Tours leave every hour on the hour. The temperature in the mine is 50 degrees, so bring a coat.

A gold-bearing stream runs from the mine's entrance. An instructor will teach you how to pan for gold.

COLORADO

*Topaz -
Topaz Mountain
Gem Mine*

REGION:
Southwest

ADDRESS:
2010 Wold Ave.
Colorado Springs, Colorado 80909
(719) 596-5492

DIRECTIONS:
Take Interstate 25 to Colorado Springs and go west on U.S. Highway 24 (Exit 141).
Proceed 39.1 miles (through Woodland Park) to County Road 77. Turn right, go 6.7
miles to Matukat Road and turn right. It is 2.3 miles to the mine.

SEASON:
May 15 to September 15

HOURS:
8:30 a.m. to 5:00 p.m., daily

COST:
Pay by the bucket
One bucket — $10.00

WHAT TO BRING:
All equipment is provided by the mine including instructions.

INFORMATION:
The Topaz Mountain Gem Mine boasts of having the richest unsalted material in
the country. You will be allowed to screen your own material from previously dug
buckets of dirt. Due to insurance and liability, you are not allowed to dig your own.

Fine, gem-quality topaz is found daily. The mine guarantees you will find topaz.
Gem-quality blue, pink, and colorless topaz are found here. Sporadic bi-colored
pieces of pink and blue topaz are occasionally discovered. Phenakite inclusions are
also occasionally found in the topaz. Quartz and feldspar are found at the mine as
well.

Rough and faceted topaz are for sale on the premises. The mine can arrange to
have your finds cut.

Camping facilities are available two miles away at the Stage Stop Campground.
This establishment has electric hookups, hot showers and a dumping station.

NEW MEXICO

Peridot - The Kilbourne Hole

REGION:
Southwest

ADDRESS:
New Mexico Bureau of Mines & Mineral Resources
New Mexico Tech
801 Leroy Place
Socorro, New Mexico 84796
(505) 835-5420

DIRECTIONS:
This is a desert area, so be prepared. It is 60 miles from El Paso, Texas, to Kilbourne Hole, New Mexico. The specific directions are available for a small fee from the New Mexico Bureau of Mines & Mineral Resources by calling the number above. Directions are lengthy and since this is a desert area, you should have the complete directions in hand before setting out.

SEASON:
Open all year round

HOURS:
Daylight

COST:
Free

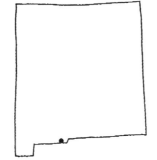

WHAT TO BRING:
Standard tools are needed. Take along a shovel, rock hammer, collecting buckets and a pick.

INFORMATION:
This destination is for rockhounds with experience in the desert. Summer temperatures exceed 100 degrees and winter temperatures are below freezing. Spring and fall may be hot or wet and bring intense thunderstorms. Rattlesnakes are active in late spring. Kilbourne Hole is on public land managed by the Bureau of Land Management. When planning a trip, let a friend know where you plan to be and when you will leave and return. Then check in when you get back home.

The Kilbourne Hole is a volcanic crater. Peridot appearance coincides with volcanic explosions 25,000 years ago. The crystals are small and may appear in the sand, however their origin is in "xenolith bombs" which are elliptical rocks 2 to 40 centimeters in length. The exterior of these "bombs" vary; the interior is full of green to greenish-yellow crystals. Peridot found here is of gem quality.

NEW MEXICO

Agate, Geode, Jasper - Rockhound State Park

REGION:
Southwest

ADDRESS:
P.O. Box 1064
Deming, New Mexico 88031
(505) 546-6182

DIRECTIONS:
Rockhound State Park is located outside of Deming, New Mexico. Take State Highway 549 east 6 miles from where it intersects State Highway 11 in the middle of town. Then proceed south 5.9 miles on State Highway 143, following the well-marked signs to the park.

SEASON:
Open all year

HOURS:
7:30 a.m. until sundown

COST:
$3.00 — admission fee for day use
$7.00 — admission fee including tent camping
$11.00 — admission fee including electric hookups

WHAT TO BRING:
General mining supplies, camping supplies, food and beverages.

INFORMATION:
Located on the west side of the Little Florida Mountains, the 250-acre Rockhound State Park allows visitors to dig for agates, jaspers, geodes, and other semiprecious minerals. Jaspers found here are yellow, pink, orange, brown, and varigated. Thundereggs and geode nodules are filled with agate or common opal, or a combination of both. They may be hollow, lined with crystals, or solid. Perlite and quartz crystals are also found along with numerous other minerals. Visitors are welcome to take 15 to 20 pounds of material from the park.

The landscape is rough, with loose rocks and inconspicuous drop-offs, so watch your step. There are numerous trails, throughout the park. As with all things, the easy access trails offer the least opportunities and specimens. You'll have to work a bit and travel the extra mile to find extraordinary rocks and minerals.

The camping area is used as a base camp for exploration and collection activities and offers restrooms, dump stations, and showers.

NEW MEXICO

Azurite, Barite, Pyrite -
Nitt Mine &
North Graphic
Mine

REGION:
Southwest

ADDRESS:
Bill's Gem & Mineral Shop
c/o William Dobson
P.O. Box 104
Magdalena, New Mexico 87825
(505) 854-2236

DIRECTIONS:
From Albuquerque, New Mexico take Interstate 25 south to Exit 150 (Exit 147 from Truth or Consequences). Take U.S. Highway 60 west 28 miles to Magdalena, New Mexico. Bill's Gem and Mineral Shop is on U.S. Highway 60 on Magdalena's main street which is the corner of First and Pine. The shop is in a large house next to the Ponderosa Restaurant and the Women of the Mountain Inn.

SEASON:
Open all year round.
The mine may be closed due to poor weather conditions.

HOURS:
8:00 a.m. to 5:00 p.m., seven days a week

COST:
$3.00 per person per day, with a 20-pound limit.

WHAT TO BRING:
Standard mining tools may be helpful, but are not necessary to find specimens. Bring sun protection, food and drink.

INFORMATION:
Nice pyrite specimens can be found on the tailings piles of these two mines. You will be digging in the tailings piles for all sorts of minerals. There is copper, azurite, bornite, iron ores and some blue smithsonite. The Nitt Mine is best for pyrite and the Graphic Mine is often better for smithsonite, azurite, and sphalerite in small quantities. You will need to be patient with your searching and digging.

Call ahead to make sure that you can gain access to the mine(s). You will need a key to get by the two gates to access the mine. Mr. Dobson accommodates groups and checks on individuals mining alone. You may camp at the site, but there are no facilities. Bring a Coleman stove. Drought conditions make open fires a hazard.

ARIZONA

Fire Agates -
Black Hills Rockhound
Area

REGION:
Southwest

ADDRESS:
Bureau of Land Management, Safford Field Office
711 14th Avenue
Safford, Arizona 85546
(520) 428-4040

DIRECTION:
The Black Hills Rockhound Area is located due east of Phoenix, near the New Mexico border, between Safford and Clifton, Arizona. From Safford take U.S. Highway 70 east to U.S. Highway 191. Travel northeast 10.5 miles to milepost marker 141. Just past the marker take BLM Road 3829 to the left, approximately 1 mile, to the register site.

SEASON:
Open all year round

HOURS:
Daylight

COST:
Free

WHAT TO BRING:
You need standard mining equipment and a quarter-inch, mesh sifting screen. Bring food and all drinking water.

INFORMATION:
Fire agate is considered a gemstone because of its unique color and fire similar to the luster of a pearl. Fire agates are less costly than fire opals, of superior hardness and will not fade. Stop at the BLM office to register and obtain directions and rules. Fire agates can be found on the surface, while more superior specimens require some digging. Digging and sifting dirt is the technique used. Fire agates are reddish brown in color and found with fire sometimes visible.

The access road is rough and not appropriate for trailers or passenger cars. Like all Southwest areas, rattlesnakes can be found here, especially in the summer months. Rock slides, ledges and old buildings present hazards. Be sure to fill all your digging holes before you leave. If camping in primitive areas, be certain to control and thoroughly extinguish all fires.

ARIZONA

Metal Detecting for Gold -
Prescott National Forest
Lynx Creek

REGION:
Southwest

ADDRESS:
Bradshaw Ranger District
2230 E. Highway 69
Prescott, Arizona 86301
(520) 445-7253

DIRECTIONS:
From Prescott, Arizona take State Highway 69 east to Walker Road. Then take Walker Road south to Lynx Lake Recreation Area.

SEASON:
Open all year round

HOURS:
Daylight

COST:
Free to recreational miners

WHAT TO BRING:
You are permitted to bring hand tools, non-motorized gold mining equipment and a metal detector.

INFORMATION:
This area is a good place to search for gold nuggets. You can pan for gold in the creek or search the land for nuggets. The district is supervised by the U.S. Forest Service. Only gold pans, metal detectors and hand tools are permitted in your search. Do not disturb the natural features of this land.

Pick and shovel excavations may only be done in conjunction with gold panning and metal detecting and must be done below the high-water mark of the stream channels. Excavations must not damage roots or live vegetation. Specific rules and maps are available from the address above.

Camping is primitive. You may camp at this site for up to 14 days. The following regulations apply to camping here — pack out what you bring in; do not wash dishes or yourself in Lynx Creek; no toilets are available (bury your waste 100 feet from the creek); control your campfires.

UTAH

REGION:
Southwest

ADDRESS:
Moab Rock Shop
600 North Main
Moab, Utah 84532
(801) 259-7312

DIRECTIONS:
The Moab Rock Shop is located on U.S. Highway 191, which is Main Street in Moab, Utah.

SEASON:
April 15 to September 30

HOURS:
9:00 a.m. to 5:00 p.m.

COST:
$75.00 per person per day
$50.00 per person per half day

WHAT TO BRING:
All equipment is supplied by the outfitters, even your lunch and drinks.

INFORMATION:
   Lin Ottinger's Tours offer a wide variety of scenic tours and hiking. Photographer, geologist and naturalist, Lin Ottinger is known as the dinosaur man. Brigham Young University even named a dinosaur after him, *Iguanandon Ottinger.*

   The area around Moab, Utah, is extraordinary with deep canyons, towering red cliffs, buttes, and balanced rock and natural stone arches all carved by wind and time. Tours for fossils and rock hunting can be planned to fit your desires. Collecting is permitted on the tours except in the national parks. Lin Ottinger can assist you in shipping your specimens. Some fossils found on the tours include trilobites, coral, clams and petrified wood.

   Mr. Ottinger invites you to come early and browse around the museum. Enjoy the collection of dinosaur bones, fossils, rare minerals and gemstones from the Moab area. Call to make reservations.

NEVADA

*Opal Mine -
Rainbow Ridge*

REGION:
Southwest

ADDRESS:
P.O. Box 97
Denio, Nevada 89404
(602) 945-2262 (before 5/10), (702) 941-0270 (after 5/10)

DIRECTIONS:
From Denio Junction, travel west on State Highway 140 for 22.5 miles to a dirt road on the left (the turnoff is 90 miles from Lakeview, Oregon). Travel on the dirt road 2.5 miles to the CCC Camp. Signs from the CCC Camp will lead you the final 5 miles to the mine. The last 7.5 miles are dirt and gravel roads.

SEASON:
Memorial Day through September

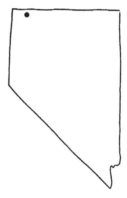

HOURS:
8:00 a.m. to 4:00 p.m.
Closed Tuesday and Thursday

COST:
Adults — $20.00 per day to dig on tailings piles
Children 10 to 15 years — $10.00

WHAT TO BRING:
Standard mining tools including tweezers and a spray bottle.

INFORMATION:
The opal found here is some of the most beautiful in the world. Most of the common opal found at the Rainbow Ridge Opal Mine is black, white or wood opal. All of the opal found here occurs in wood-opal combinations or wood casts. The mine allows digging on tailings piles only. New material is bulldozed several times a week and dumped on the tailings piles.

The petrified wood and opal occuring here was once part of a pine forest. Rare opalized pine cones have been found. Long ago the Roebling Black Opal was found here. It is 18 ounces and is now owned by the Smithsonian Institute.

Finding opal involves knowing what to look for and a bit of good luck. The mine suggests you stop by the rock shop to see what the specimens you are searching for look like. Some minerals are for sale. There is no overnight camping at the mine, but it is available at the CCC Camp five miles away.

NEVADA

Opal Mine -
The Royal Peacock
Opal Mine

REGION:
Southwest

ADDRESS:
P.O. Box 55
Denio, Nevada 89404
(702) 941-0374

DIRECTIONS:
From Denio, Nevada take State Highway 140 west for 25 miles. Turn left at the Bureau of Land Management sign onto a dirt road and follow the signs to the Royal Peacock Opal Mine. The CCC Campground is 2.5 miles down this road. The mines are 7 miles farther along the dirt road.

SEASON:
May 15 to October 15, weather permitting

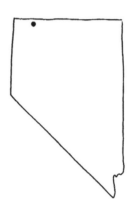

HOURS:
8:00 a.m. to 4:00 p.m.

COST:
$50.00 — for bank digging
$20.00 — for tailings digging
Camping: RV is $12.00 per night,
$3.00 for other types of camping.

WHAT TO BRING:
You will need equipment for opal mining listed in the front of the book on page eight.

INFORMATION:
    You can keep all that you find at the Royal Peacock Opal Mine. Black opals are found here, as well as some fire and wood opals. This area was once a forest. The trees fell and over time, buried in silica, became opals of extraordinary beauty. Mining of opals has taken place in this valley since the 1900s. Since then, millions of dollars of opals have been mined in this region. Over 200 private claims are mined here. In 1992, a man found a opalized log weighing 130 pounds. Several of this region's opals are on display at the Smithsonian in Washington, D.C.
    You can dig in the banks or in the tailings pile. No rock hammers are permitted. There is a full service opal shop on-site with equipment, specimens and cut stones. Full RV hookups, furnished trailers and tent camping sites are available. The camp has a shower and laundry facility. Call in advance for reservations to camp.

NEVADA

REGION:
Southwest

ADDRESS:
Bureau of Land Management - Ely District Office
H.C. 33, Box 33500
Ely, Nevada 89301
(702) 289-4865

DIRECTIONS:
Garnet Fields Rockhound Area is located on U.S. Highway 50 near Ely, Nevada. From Ely, at the traffic light at the junction of U.S. Highway 93 and U.S. Highway 50, take U.S. Highway 50 west 6.4 miles. The access road to the area is .25 mile north of the turnoff to Ruth, Nevada. Take the access road 3.1 miles to Garnet Hill. The access road is winding and somewhat steep, but is suitable to all types of vehicles. Garnet Hill is a 1280-acre site on public lands.

SEASON:
Open year round, weather permitting

HOURS:
Daylight

COST:
Free

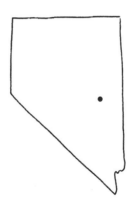

WHAT TO BRING:
You'll need standard mining equipment as well as a knife, screwdriver and prybar.

INFORMATION:
 This area is famous for its dark red garnets found in volcanic rock. These garnets are of the Almandine variety and are dark red. Most are flawed, but some gem-quality stones are found.
 Garnets can be found by searching the surface and drainage areas for dark colored stones that have weathered from their host rock or by breaking open garnet-bearing rock with a pick or hammer to reveal the gems. The garnets usually occur as a single crystal inside air pockets (vugs) within the volcanic rock. Look for rock with veins of quartz. Garnets found inside a vug must be carefully extracted with a knife or similar tool. Be careful, as the garnets are hard, but brittle and may shatter.
 Limited space for tent camping and small RVs is available. Also visible from this site is the large, open-pit copper mine and multi-colored, waste rock dumps at the nearby Robinson Mining District.

CALIFORNIA

Fire Agates -
Opal Hill Mine

REGION:
Southwest

ADDRESS:
Nancy Hill
c/o Opal Hill Mine
P.O. Box 497
Palo Verde, California 92266

DIRECTIONS:
Blythe, California is located off of Interstate 10 in southeast California, near the
Arizona border. From Blythe, take State Highway 78 south to Palo Verde, California.
Continue on State Highway 78 to Fourth Street and travel west through town for
about 1 mile. Continue on Fourth Street as it curves to the right, heads out of town
and towards the mountains, traveling approximatley 9 miles to the mine. Take a left
turn into the mine office.

SEASON:
November 1 to May 1

HOURS:
Daylight

COST:
$10.00 per person per day

WHAT TO BRING:
Take a rock hammer, chisel, whisk broom,
gloves, goggles and a long-handled screwdriver.
Bring plenty of drinking water for this arid
climate.

INFORMATION:
    This is a wonderful place to find quality fire agates and is certainly a bargain for
the price of admission. The fire agates appear somewhat orange in color and resemble opals with flashes of internal color. In addition to the fire agates you can find
chalcedony, quartz crystals, apatite, barite and various other minerals.
    Some hardrock mining is necessary. The mine owners are very helpful and will
make sure you get the most out of your efforts. It does take effort to remove the
fiery gemstones from the tough host rock.
    Camping is available at the mine. There are also some trailers here for your use.
No reservations are required. Dogs are welcome as well, so bring your whole family.

CALIFORNIA  *Gold Panning - Keysville Recreation Area*

REGION:
Southwest

ADDRESS:
Bureau of Land Management
3801 Pegasus Drive
Bakersfield, California 93308-6837
(805) 391-6000

DIRECTIONS:
From Los Angeles go north on Interstate 5 to Kern County. Take State Highway 99 north. At Bakersfield, take State Highway 178 to Lake Isabella. Turn left on State Highway 155. The Keysville Recreation Area is approximately .5 mile.

SEASON:
Open all year round

HOURS:
Daylight

COST:
Free

WHAT TO BRING:
Bring standard mining and gold mining equipment. Sluice boxes and dredges up to three inches are permitted. You must have a permit to use a dredge. Bring your own food, camping supplies and drinking water.

INFORMATION:
The Keysville Recreation Area is located on the Kern River and is open to the public for placer mining. Please be aware of private claims and do not trespass. Placer gold is found in this river. The river is rocky, with some steep grades and dangerous currents. Use of metal detectors is allowed. High banking is not allowed. Best results have been made by searching the cracks and crevices in the river bedrock.

This site is popular in the summer, especially on weekends because of its proximity to Los Angeles. Camping is primitive, but portable toilets are provided in the summer. Camping is limited to 14 days per month, 28 days per year.

CALIFORNIA

*Moonstones -
Moonstone Beach*

REGION:
Southwest

ADDRESS:
Cambria Chamber of Commerce
767 Main Street
Cambria, California 93428
(805) 927-3624

DIRECTIONS:
Moonstone Beach is in Cambria, California.
From State Highway 1, take Exit SR 1 at Windsor
Boulevard. Take Moonstone Beach Drive to the beach.

SEASON:
Open all year round

HOURS:
Daylight

COST:
Free

WHAT TO BRING:
You'll want a pail or other collecting container to hold your moonstones.

INFORMATION:
   Rock hunting and beach combing are popular pastimes here. A variety of stones can be found on the beach, including California "jade," agates and moonstones. Moonstones are a cloudy, milky quartz. When polished, moonstones are clear with an internal fiery glow. Agates have a translucent look and the stone may have an orange-peel texture. Expect the beach to be somewhat rocky and the water is often chilly.
   For day use there are two parks: Leffingwell Landings and Shamel Park. Both parks offer restrooms, picnic areas, and beach access. The area has numerous hotels. This beach town has much to do, including shopping, whale watching and visiting Hearst Castle.

CALIFORNIA

REGION:
Southwest

ADDRESS:
Off Pacific Coast Highway (1)
California
No phone

DIRECTION:
California Pacific coastal beaches around
Cape San Martin, Jade Cove and Sand Dollar Beach
on State Highway 1.

SEASON:
Open all year round

HOURS:
Daylight

COST:
Free

WHAT TO BRING:
Bring a bucket or other carrying container. The water is cold and the beaches rugged, rocky and beautiful. Wear clothing appropriate for the windy Northern California beaches.

INFORMATION:
Green jade and serpentine can be found in these areas: Cape San Martin, Jade Cove and Sand Dollar Beach. The Cape San Martin Beach access is from State Highway 1 to Willow Creek Bridge. The best area for searching is from the north side of the point to the Willow Creek Bridge. Another site is less than two miles north of Cape San Martin at Jade Cove. Access is marked by a small sign. The turnoff is narrow but can accommodate two or three cars.

One-half mile north has the best marked access and the best amenities including restrooms and picnic tables. This is Sand Dollar Beach. Note the cliffs next to the access steps. They are green serpentine flaked with gold. There is a campground across State Highway 1 called Plaskett Creek.

CALIFORNIA

*Gold Panning -
Gold Prospecting
Expeditions &
Adventure Trips*

REGION:
Southwest

ADDRESS:
18170 Main Street
P.O. Box 1040
Jamestown, California 95327
(209) 984-4653

DIRECTIONS:
Located between Sonora and Oakdale on State Highway 49 in Jamestown, California.

SEASON:
Open 364 days a year(closed Christmas day)

HOURS:
Daylight

COST:
Adults — $3.00
Children — $1.00
Trips and courses cost extra

WHAT TO BRING:
All supplies are provided.

INFORMATION:
    The Gold Prospecting Expeditions and Adventure Trips is just what it claims to be and more. They have an 1849 gold mining camp set up as a living history exhibit. There is a costumed prospector who will explain and demonstrate the workings of the gold pans, cradles and long-toms. He will also tell you all about the miner's lifestyle back in 1849. The proprietors ask you to keep a sharp eye out for claim jumpers. Bring a carrot for Molly, the camp mule.

    They run educational school trips, family outings, courses, helicopter trips and white water rafting trips. Course topics include a three-day prospecting class, a high banking class, a one-day dredging trip and an electronic prospecting class. They even arrange weddings.

    If you want to prospect or you are looking for adventure, this is the place to find some gold. You will find something for everyone from the beginning miner to the expert prospector.

CALIFORNIA

Gold Panning -
Hidden Treasure
Gold Mine

REGION:
Southwest

ADDRESS:
P.O. Box 28, Washington & Main Streets
Columbia, California 95310
(209) 532-9693

DIRECTIONS:
The Hidden Treasure Gold Mine is located on the corner of Main & Washington Streets, Columbia State Historic Park in Columbia, California.

SEASON:
Open all year round. Call for winter hours, which are shortened. Regular season is March 1 to September 1.

HOURS:
9:00 a.m. to 5:00 p.m., seven days a week

COST:
Tour and Panning:
Adults — $13.00
Children and Seniors — $12.00
Tour Only:
Adults — $8.00
Children and Seniors — $7.00

WHAT TO BRING:
All tools are supplied by the mine. The mine does have a mine supply store.

INFORMATION:
The Hidden Treasure Gold Mine is the only active working gold mine open to the public. Discovered in 1879, it still produces gold today. The mine offers several panning opportunities. Don't miss out. Try your luck!

Guided tours leave from the Matelot Gold Mine Supply Store. The office opens at 10:00 a.m. and tours begin at 10:30 a.m. You will travel through 800 feet of tunnel to see what a working mine looks like. During your tour of this hardrock mine you can see veins of gold and quartz in the mine walls. The mine temperature is 54 degrees. Bring a coat.

CALIFORNIA

Gold Prospecting - Roaring Camp Mining Company

REGION:
Southwest

ADDRESS:
P.O. Box 278
Pine Grove, California 95665
(209) 296-4100

DIRECTIONS:
From Sacramento take U.S. Highway 50 to State Highway 16 (Jackson Highway).
Take a right on State Highway 49 continuing south to Jackson. Take State Highway
88 east until you come to Pine Grove. Follow it to the camp.

SEASON:
May 1 to September 30

HOURS:
Tours begin at 8:30 a.m., 10:00 a.m., and 2:30 p.m.
Tours are four hours in length.

COST:
Cost for one to two persons is $370.00 per week,
this includes a cabin and use of the facilities.

WHAT TO BRING:
Take along standard gold mining gear including a dredge and
sluice box. The camp will also sell or rent prospecting equipment.

INFORMATION:
   The camp offers gold panning, dredging and sluicing. The area is also good for
the rockhound looking for crystals, jade, jaspers, river rubies, and garnets. A guide is
available for fishing and to help you with prospecting for gold. Swimming is also
available. Roaring Camp offers a roaring good barbecue on Saturday nights.
   Cabins cost $370.00 per week for one or two persons, $135.00 for each additional person. Family rates for two people are $370.00, while each additional person
under 18 years of age is $100.00. The mining tour takes you to old mines, allows
you to pan for gold, collect minerals and visit the artifact museum.

CALIFORNIA

Gold Panning -
Gold Country
Prospecting

REGION:
Southwest

ADDRESS:
3119 Turner Street
Placerville, California 95667
(916) 622-2484

DIRECTIONS:
The area of prospecting varies. You will be prospecting in a stream or creek in the Placerville area which is located northeast of Sacramento on U.S. Highway 50.

SEASON:
Spring, summer and fall

HOURS:
Three-hour trips scheduled during daylight hours.

COST:
Three-hour trips are:
Adults — $40.00
Children under 12 — $20.00
Children under 7 — Free

WHAT TO BRING:
All the equipment will be supplied. If you would like to bring your own equipment you may bring standard gold mining gear. Bring an extra pair of socks and shoes. Your feet will definitely get wet.

INFORMATION:
   A guide will teach folks how to prospect for gold in area creeks and streams. Groups are 10 people or less to maximize the learning experience. You will learn gold panning and how to use a sluice box on your trip. The trip takes about three hours. The water is cold and you will definitely get wet, so bring a change of clothing.
   The terrain is beautiful and the work invigorating. The guide will tell you stories of the glory of the California gold rush and enlighten you with some local history.
   This is a great way to learn the ropes with your own expert guide. Greenhorns are welcome and you keep all the gold you find. Gold Country Prospecting guarantees that no one will go home empty handed.

CALIFORNIA

Gold Panning - Marshall Gold Discovery State Historic Park

REGION:
Southwest

ADDRESS:
P.O. Box 265
310 Back Street
Coloma, California 95613
(916) 622-3470

DIRECTIONS:
Coloma, California is located east of Sacramento. From Interstate 80, exit at Auburn and take State Highway 49 south 20 miles to Coloma.

SEASON:
Open all year round

HOURS:
8:00 a.m. to sunset

COST:
$5.00 admission per car

WHAT TO BRING:
Bring standard gold mining equipment.
Sluicing and dredging are not permitted here.

INFORMATION:

This is the site of Sutter's Mill, where James Marshall found gold and started the California Gold Rush in 1848. Now a historic park is located here. Included within the park is a gold museum and replicas of buildings including Sutter's Saw Mill, a blacksmith shop, a Chinese store and much more.

The mining exhibit contains examples of the equipment used by the '49ers and depicts gold mining methods such as placer, hardrock and hydraulic mining. This area was so gold laden that the business district of Coloma was torn down so the area could be mined for gold.

A 45-minute walking tour will take you by all of the sites and to the spot where James Marshall discovered gold. Activities include four walking tours of one-third to one and one-half miles in length. Gold panning in the recreational gold panning area is available here on the streambed.

CALIFORNIA

*Gold Panning -
Union Flat Casual
Mining Area*

REGION:
Southwest

ADDRESS:
15924 Highway 49
Camptonville, California 95922
(916) 478-6253

DIRECTIONS:
Union Flat Casual Mining Area is located in Tahoe National Forest in the Downieville
Ranger District. Turn right off State Highway 49, approximately 5 miles east of
Downieville, California, into the Union Flat Campground.

SEASON:
Panning: Open all year round
Dredging: June 1 to October 15

HOURS:
Daylight

COST:
Free

WHAT TO BRING:
Standard gold mining gear. Dredges up to four inches
are permitted. Bring your own food, camping supplies
and drinking water.

INFORMATION:
   Union Flat Casual Mining Area is located on federal land, overseen by the U.S.
Forest Service. It has produced some nice gold flakes in the past. Camping is permitted in the campground area only, which has a 14-day limit. Panning is permitted
year round. Dredging requires a permit available from the California Department of
Fish and Game at (916) 225-2300. Dredges up to four inches are permitted.
   Casual Mining Rules from the forest service were established to protect the land
and reduce conflicts with other users. Rules include — mine only the wet areas of
stream; no bank mining or disturbing roots of any plants; hand tools, only; do not
build dams; leave the site as you found it, and no jet or nozzle mining.

CALIFORNIA

Gold Panning - Golden Caribou Claims

REGION:
Southwest

ADDRESS:
Caribou Corner Campground
P.O. Box 300
Belden, California 95915
(916) 283-0956

INFORMATION:
From Belden, California, take State Highway 70 to Caribou Road. The Golden Caribou is approximately 1 mile north up the road.

SEASON:
Open all year round

HOURS:
Daylight

COST:
Recreational miners mine for free. Professional miners pay a 15% royalty. Some claims are $10.00 per person, per day.

WHAT TO BRING:
Bring standard mining and gold mining equipment, sluice boxes, dredges and high bankers. Some supplies are available for rent.

INFORMATION:
Caribou Corner has many claims that are available for beginners to experts. In 1993, the largest nugget found was a six and one-half ounce nugget of gold. All claims contain fine gold. Most claims have also produced some nuggets. Caribou Corner guarantees that you will find gold.

They offer full-day training sessions, which will teach you the basics of searching for gold and how to use dredges and high bankers. Sessions cost $50.00, other training is also available.

Caribou Corner Campground has 20 campsites with full hookups. The campground has a shower facility, laundry, camp store and cafe. Rates are $14.00 for camping. Cabins are $50.00 per night.

CALIFORNIA

Gold Panning - Butte Creek Recreation Area

REGION:
Southwest

ADDRESS:
Bureau of Land Management - Redding District
355 Hemsted Drive
Redding, California 96002
(916) 224-2100

DIRECTIONS:
From Chico, California, take State Highway 32 north towards Chester. Drive past the Forest Ranch and turn right on Garland Road. Follow Garland Road to Doe Mill Road (210C) to Butte Creek Bridge. Park here to access sites 12 to 30. To reach sites 5 to 11, cross the bridge and head east, turning left at Ditch Creek Road (210-C2) which is just west of the creek.

SEASON:
Open all year round

HOURS:
Daylight

COST:
The prospecting fee is $2.50 per person per day.

WHAT TO BRING:
Bring standard mining and gold mining equipment. Sluice boxes and dredges up to four inches are permitted. Bring your own food, camping supplies and drinking water. This is a national forest and camping is primitive.

INFORMATION:
Butte Creek is a good place to try your panning skills and find some placer gold. Butte Creek has two individual places to prospect. The area has 30 sites. Sites 1 to 4 are not recommended to prospect because it requires crossing private land. Sites 5 to 11 are the most popular because they are flat to allow easy access to camping nearby. Sites numbered 12 to 30 are also available for prospecting.

A BLM permit is required at this unique site for all forms of intrusive mineral collecting such as dredging, pumping, sluicing and extensive panning. Dredging also requires a California Dredge Permit available from the California Department of Fish and Game at (916) 225-2300.

CALIFORNIA

Gold Panning - Big Flat Recreation Area

REGION:
Southwest

ADDRESS:
Big Bar Ranger District
Route 1, Box 10
Big Bar, California 96010
(916) 623-6106

DIRECTIONS:
From Weaverville, California, take State Highway 299 west for 22 miles to the Big Flat Recreation Area.

SEASON:
Open all year round

HOURS:
Daylight

COST:
Free

WHAT TO BRING:
Bring standard mining and gold mining equipment. Sluice boxes and dredges up to four inches are permitted. Bring your own food and drinking water.

INFORMATION:
The Big Flat Recreation Area is located in the Shasta - Trinity National Forest. This is the only area in the forest which is open to the public for gold panning and dredging. No permit is needed for panning in this area. If you are dredging you do need a California State Fish & Game Dredge Permit obtained by calling (916) 225-2300. This area has good access for prospecting and good gold potential.

Camping is permitted for up to 14 days in this primitive area at no cost. There is also an RV park one-half mile east of the Big Flat Recreation Area which has showers and supplies available.

MONTANA

REGION:
Northwest

ADDRESS:
Custer County
Route 1, Box 1206A
Hardin, Montana 59034
(406) 665-1671

DIRECTIONS:
Montana agates can be found along the Yellowstone River parallel to Interstate 94 and State Highway 16 from Custer to Sidney.

SEASON:
Spring and summer

HOURS:
Daylight

COST:
Free

WHAT TO BRING:
You will need a small shovel or other hand-held tools and a bucket to carry your finds. Bring your own food and drink. We also recommend you bring a change of clothes.

INFORMATION:
Montana agate is one of the official gemstones of the state. You may also find petrified wood, colored jaspers and fossils. The Montana agates are called plume or moss agates for the interesting formations within the stone which resemble plumes and moss growth. Good quality specimens are beautiful and valuable.

Agates are found in the terrace gravel high above the river. These deposits are difficult to access, as they are mainly on private land. Additional specimens are located along the river in gravel deposits. These stones are much more approachable. Agates found in the area are translucent, meaning that some light does pass through them. They often appear cloudy when found in nature. Colors vary and can be white, tan or bluish.

Acquire permission from the owner if you want to collect on private land. Contact local rock shops for guide service or trips for searching out these gems.

MONTANA

Petrified Wood - Gallatin National Forest

REGION:
Northwest

ADDRESS:
P.O. Box 5
Gardiner, Montana 59030
(406) 848-7375

DIRECTION:
From Emigrant, Montana, take U.S. Highway 89 south for 15 miles. Then take Tom Miner Basin Road west for 7 miles. Go to the campground near the head of a beautiful mountain valley in Gallatin National Forest.

SEASON:
Spring and fall

HOURS:
Daylight

COST:
Free with permit to enter the park.

WHAT TO BRING:
No equipment is needed or permitted.

INFORMATION:
The petrified forest is between 35- and 55-million-years old. This forest is worth a visit because of it's natural beauty. Collecting opportunities are extremely limited. The park rangers ask that you stop at the self-serve permit station at the Tom Miner Petrified Forest entrance of the national forest. You are allowed to collect only one sample of two inches by two inches by three inches. The piece must be loose on the ground. Digging is not permitted.

This forest was established to preserve the fossils and petrified wood. Trails have been constructed for visitors to see first hand petrified specimens. The trail is one-half mile long. Hiking is permitted throughout the forest.

MONTANA

REGION:
Northwest

ADDRESS:
P.O. Box 173
Alder, Montana 59710
No phone

DIRECTIONS:
The Red Rock Mine is located 1.5 miles east of Alder, on State Highway 287, between Alder and Virginia City.

SEASON:
April 1 to October 31

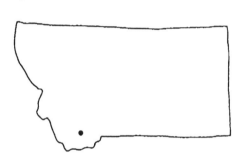

HOURS:
10:00 a.m. to 6:00 p.m.

COST:
To dig — $15.00 per day
By the bucket — $10.00
Sample bags — $3.00

WHAT TO BRING:
You will need a spray bottle with water, a film container to hold your stones and long tweezers to pluck up your stones. Bring work gloves, shovel and a pick, if you plan to dig your own dirt. The mine will rent some equipment.

INFORMATION:
The proprietors at the Red Rock Mine are clearing an area of concentrated, pond bank gravel. This gravel was a waste product of gold dredges used during the gold rush days. Miners at the Red Rock Mine are finding red and pink rhodolite and gray and purple corundum (sapphires). Gem-quality garnets in colors ranging from light pink to deep blood red are also found here.

The mine also sells Montana gold and sapphire gravel from other mines along with gems, jewelry, rocks and minerals. Gravel can also be mail ordered in bags ranging in price from $16.00 to $60.00.

You and your family can camp at the KOA Campground, which is only one mile west of the Red Rock Mine.

MONTANA

Quartz Crystals -
Crystal Park

REGION:
Northwest

ADDRESS:
Dillion Ranger District Office
Beaverhead National Forest
Dillon, Montana 59725
(406) 683-3900

DIRECTIONS:
From Butte, Montana, take Interstate 90 west to Interstate 15 south. Drive 15 miles south to the town of Divide. Turn west onto State Highway 43 toward Wise River and travel 12 miles. Past the town of Wise River, turn south on a two-lane, paved road called the Wise River-Polaris National Scenic Byway. Go south 27 miles into the Pioneer Mountains. The park is on the south side of the road.

SEASON:
May 15 to September 30

HOURS:
Daylight

COST:
Free

WHAT TO BRING:
Standard mining tools, plus a quarter-inch mesh screen, and a container to hold your crystals.

INFORMATION:
   Dig your own quartz crystals and amethyst on this 40-acre site within the national forest. Use hand tools and a quarter-inch screen to sift the sandy soil in search for treasure. There is a short walk from the parking area to the mine site, so bring a pack to carry your tools. A volunteer host is available to answer questions during the summer.
   The quartz crystals have six sides and resemble prisms. They are clear and cloudy, white, gray or purple. Crystals range from thumb size to several inches in length. Only hand tools are permitted for digging. No claims may be staked. No tunneling or working on vertical walls higher than four feet is allowed. The camp is closed overnight. Be prepared for cool weather, because it rains and snows at these higher elevations even in the summer.

MONTANA

Sapphires - Spokanne Bar Sapphire Mine

REGION:
Northwest

ADDRESS:
5360 Castles Road
Helena, Montana 59602
(406) 227-8989

DIRECTIONS:
From Helena, take York Road east 8 miles to Hart Drive. Bear right at milepost marker 8 onto Hart Drive to the Spokanne Bar Sapphire Mine. Follow the signs. If you pass Deal Lane you have passed Hart Drive.

SEASON:
April 1 until the first snowfall

HOURS:
9:00 a.m. to 5:00 p.m., seven days a week

COST:
$25.00 — per gallon bucket of concentrate
$36.25 — per person per day to dig
$52.50 — per couple to dig for 8 hours maximum

WHAT TO BRING:
Equipment is available. If you are digging your own dirt bring a shovel, quarter-inch screen (available there), whisk broom, prybar, screwdriver and gloves. To sort your sapphires you need a pair of tweezers, a spray bottle and a container with a lid.

INFORMATION:
The Spokanne Bar Sapphire Mine has beautifully colored stones varying from white, to green, to light blue. Sapphires of a half carat up to ten carats are fairly common. The largest sapphire found here was 155 carats. Minerals frequently collected here include moss agate, petrified wood, fossils, mammoth teeth, jasper, hematite and lizard rock. Also found, but extremely rare, are diamonds, topaz, citrine and ruby.

You may dig your own dirt here in an open pit or buy it by the bucket. The staff will help you learn how to screen, sift and concentrate your dirt and find the sapphires. There is a rock shop at the mine. Gold prospectors dig here for flake and nugget gold. This entire area was once a gold prospecting area. The sapphires were passed over in the search for gold.

MONTANA

Sapphires - L♦E Ranch Outfitters

REGION:
Northwest

ADDRESS:
Box 885
Clinton, Montana 59825
(406) 825-6295

DIRECTIONS:
The L♦E ("L Diamond E") Ranch Outfitters is located east of Missoula, just off Interstate 90, at Exit 126. Take Rock Creek Road northeast to the ranch.

SEASON:
Summer pack trips leave late June through mid-September.

HOURS:
Call for information

COST:
$175.00 per person for summer pack trips,
four-day minimum

WHAT TO BRING:
All supplies for sapphire mining will be provided by the L♦E Ranch Outfitters. For more information on what to pack and information on the trips available please call the L♦E Ranch Outfitters.

INFORMATION:
The L♦E Ranch Outfitters offer pack trips to suit many needs. Among the fishing, hunting, photography and horseback riding pack trips are the sapphire mining pack trips.

You may work the claim for sapphires, hike or trail ride. The mining consists of digging dirt, sifting through the dirt and then sorting the concentrate. The trip to the mine is breathtakingly beautiful.

The trip consists of a 32-mile ride from the ranch to the trailhead, then an eleven-mile ride on horseback to the sapphire camp. At camp you are housed in a nine-foot by nine-foot, summer tent with foam mattresses. An outdoor shower facility and home-cooked meals are provided. The outdoor camp is set up for the entire summer and is quite comfortable.

MONTANA

Gold Panning - Libby Creek Panning Area

REGION:
Northwest

ADDRESS:
Canoe Gulch Ranger Station
12557 Highway 39
Lincoln County, Montana 59923
(406) 293-8861

DIRECTIONS:
Libby, Montana is 64 miles northwest of Kalispell, Montana. From Libby, take U.S. Highway 2 south to Libby Creek. At Libby Creek, turn right onto Bear Creek Road/ Forest Service Road 231. Travel 10 miles on the paved forest road and 8 additional miles on the same road as it turns to gravel.

SEASON:
May 15 to October 15

HOURS:
Daylight

COST:
Free

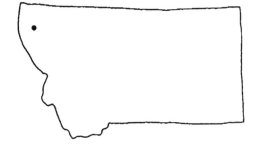

WHAT TO BRING:
You need to bring gold mining equipment. No dredges, high bankers or other motorized equipment is permitted.

INFORMATION:
   At Libby Creek Panning Area you can go and try your luck gold panning on a stream in a national forest. The creek is 30 feet from the road. You can pan all you want, but no motorized equipment, sluices or rocker boxes are allowed. This location is for those who have some experience in panning. You will not find instructors or staff to assist you, just you and the stream.

   You may camp for free in the national forest for up to 14 days. A fee campground with toilets is available one mile south at Howard Lake.

   Historic items from earlier mining days are still in evidence up the hillside. Several cabins from 1948 are also still standing. Please view, but do not disturb, these structures.

WYOMING

Fossilized Fish -
Warfield Fossil
Quarries

REGION:
Northwest

ADDRESS:
H.C.R. 61, Box 301
Thayne, Wyoming 83127
(307) 883-2445

DIRECTIONS:
The Warfield Fossil Quarries are located approximately 7 miles south of Kemmerer, Wyoming, on U.S. Highway 189. From the north, take Interstate 80 to U.S. Highway 189. Turn off U.S. Highway 189 about 12 miles north of the Bon Rico Club and follow the signs.

SEASON:
Memorial Day weekend until August 31

HOURS:
Call or write to make reservations

COST:
$35.00 per person per day

WHAT TO BRING:
All supplies and instructions are included with your mining fee. Bring your lunch and drinks. It gets very hot at mid-day so bring extra fluids.

INFORMATION:
The fish fossils found here are over 50-million-years old. You will have no trouble finding fossils. They can be found in a few hours of work. You must work slowly so you don't ruin the fossils that you reveal. Experts are on hand to instruct you. You may keep all the fossils you find, except rare specimens such as stingrays, turtles or birds.

The heavy overburden is removed by the quarry operators. You will be trying your hand at splitting large, loose blocks of limestone to discover the fossils. Your patient searching will pay off with beautiful undamaged fossils.

We suggest you start early. It is cool in the morning and a light jacket may be needed. It gets very hot by mid-day, so wear clothes in layers so you can peel out of them.

There is free camping provided for diggers at the mine. There are no hookups or utilities for campers. A restroom and hot showers are available. Children and pets are welcome.

WYOMING

*Fossilized Fish -
Ulrich's Fossil Gallery*

REGION:
Northwest

ADDRESS:
Fossil Station #308
Kemmerer, Wyoming 83101-0308
(307) 877-6466

DIRECTIONS:
The Ulrich's Fossil Gallery is located on U.S. Highway 30, 10 miles west of
Kemmerer, Wyoming.

SEASON:
Open June to Labor Day

HOURS:
9:00 a.m. to 12:00 p.m., daily

COST:
$55.00 per person per day

WHAT TO BRING:
The Ulrich's Fossil Gallery supplies you with all tools and equipment you need for
excavating and transporting your finds. Bring a camera, snack and plenty to drink.

INFORMATION:
This is a great opportunity to excavate fish fossils with a professional. Reservations are required so the owners may set you up with a staff member as a guide and instructor. The quarry is located at 7200 feet in elevation. The gallery suggests that you wear layers of clothes. It is cool in the morning and hot towards late morning. Sunglasses are highly recommended to reduce the glare.

You will be working on an ancient lake bed. Excavating is done seven days a week, weather permitting, so please call ahead. You are given three hours to quarry your fossils. You keep all specimens except those that are rare and unusual as designated by the state of Wyoming. These include, but are not limited to, gar fish, stingrays, and all mammals.

The quarry will transport you to the digging site from the quarry and furnish you with tools and equipment. Trips depart from the gallery at 9:00 a.m. unless other arrangements are made. This is an educational trip for all.

IDAHO

Opals -
The Spencer Opal Mines

REGION:
Northwest

ADDRESS:
H.C.R. 62, Box 2060
Dubois, Idaho 83423
(208) 374-5476

DIRECTIONS:
Spencer, Idaho, is just south of the Idaho - Montana line on Interstate 15. The mine is located off Interstate15 and State Highway 22 outside of Spencer. Mine headquarters are located in the town of Spencer, on the north end of Main Street at the gas station and trailer park.

SEASON:
Memorial Day weekend to September 15, weather permitting

HOURS:
9:00 a.m. to 5:00 p.m., six days a week
Closed Wednesday

COST:
$5.00 per person to mine
$4.00 per pound for material

WHAT TO BRING:
Bring a spray bottle (most important), points and chisels, a three- to four-pound rock hammer, eight-pound sledgehammer and a carrying bucket. Safety glasses are REQUIRED.

INFORMATION:
   The headquarters is open six days a week from 9:00 a.m. to 5:00 p.m. (closed Wednesday). There is more than one mine office in town, so be sure to get the right one. They carry a full line of opal-cutting supplies, rough opal and finished jewelry. They have a stockpile of mine run material that you can search through. The charge is $4.00 per pound.
   You need to obtain a permit at the mine office to dig through the pile. Water is available for washing the material, but not for drinking. You must bring your own. You will be digging in opal-bearing rock ranging in size from gravel to small boulders.

IDAHO

*Gold Panning & Rafting -
Salmon River Experience*

REGION:
Northwest

ADDRESS:
Chuck & Linda Boyd
812 Truman
Moscow, Idaho 83843
(208) 882-2385

DIRECTIONS:
You will be picked up at your hotel in Moscow, Pullman, or Lewiston, Idaho. The Salmon River Experience staff will drive you to your river guides who have the rafts ready to launch. After your trip you will be returned to your hotel in time for dinner.

SEASON:
July through August

HOURS:
Open seven days per week. Trips are four days in length.

COST:
$649 per person
Call for a flyer on other adventure trips offered.

WHAT TO BRING:
You should contact the Salmon River Experience for a complete gear list.

INFORMATION:
In the four-day trip you will raft 40 miles on the Salmon River and 20 miles on the Snake River at the bottom of Hells Canyon. You will have opportunities to see bald eagles, elk, big horn sheep, bear, otter and numerous other wild creatures. The rafts are 14- to 18-feet long and are paddled by licensed guides.

On the first day you will launch the rafts, go over safety procedures, raft through many white water rapids and enjoy the mountain scenery. On the second and third days guests will raft to historical sites, pan for gold, and explore mines worked in the late 1800s. The fourth day you will raft 20 miles down the Snake River. Louise Darby, mining history specialist, will join guests to share her knowledge of the Nez Perce Indians, early pioneers and mining in the canyon.

Your meals are very impressive and are cooked up on the riverbank for you. This trip is full of fun and adventure for all. No experience is necessary and non-swimmers are welcome. Children must be eight years or older to take this trip.

IDAHO  *Garnets & Star Garnets - 3-D Panhandle Gems & "Garnet Queen Mine"*

REGION:
Northwest

ADDRESS:
Louise Darby
P.O. Box 9082
Moscow, Idaho 83843
(208) 882-9496

DIRECTIONS:
3-D's Panhandle Gems & "Garnet Queen Mine" is on 403 Juliene Way. From Moscow, Idaho, go east on State Highway 8 and turn right at milepost marker 7. Turn left at the second place on the left.

SEASON:
May 28 to September 5

HOURS:
8:00 a.m. to 5:00 p.m.

COST:
$45.00 per person

WHAT TO BRING:
All equipment as well as instructions are supplied. You may choose to bring a container with a lid, a quarter-inch screen and hand tools. You will need to bring your own lunch and beverages. Old clothes and lace boots or sneakers are recommended.

INFORMATION:
Due to the popularity of these garnet mining trips, reservations must be made at least 30 days in advance. Your cost includes the U.S. Forest Service fee, user fee and Idaho sales tax. To get to the mining area there is a walk of three-quarter mile on an inclined road. Some of the slopes are also extremely steep.

Louise Darby will teach you where to look and a bit about how the garnets are formed. You will learn how to tell a star garnet from a facet-grade garnet. Garnets found can be the size of sand particles up to over two inches in diameter. Trips take place within the Idaho Panhandle National Forest.

Louise Darby is a licensed guide and outfitter. She will take you on a mining trip that you will never forget.

IDAHO

Garnets -
Emerald Creek Garnet
Area

REGION:
Northwest

ADDRESS:
St. Joe Ranger District
P.O. Box 407
St. Maries, Idaho 83861
(208) 245-2531

DIRECTIONS:
From St. Maries, Idaho, follow State Highway 3 south 24 miles. Take Road 447 southeast for 8 miles to the Emerald Creek Garnet Area parking area. The admission permit, information and digging area are a .5 mile hike up 281 Gulch. Carry all your equipment with you.

SEASON:
Memorial Day to Labor Day

HOURS:
9:00 a.m. to 5:00 p.m., closed Wednesday & Thursday

COST:
Adults: $10.00 per day
Children: $5.00 per day

WHAT TO BRING:
You will need a shovel, bucket, quarter-inch mesh screen for washing gravel, container with lid for garnets and a change of clothes - this is wet, muddy work.

INFORMATION:
The twelve-sided (dodecahedron) star garnets are found in only two places in the world. Crystals can range in size from a grain of sand to a golf ball or larger. Stars found here are both four-ray and six-ray. Some material is of gem quality. You may dig in designated areas only and may carry away up to five pounds of garnets. If you want more than five pounds of material you must buy another permit (limit of 30 pounds per person per year).

This location has an administration building with restrooms, visitor's information and assistance, permit sales and a garnet display. Four miles east of Emerald Creek Garnet Area is Emerald Creek Campground. The camping fee is $6.00 per night. Food, gas and other supplies are six miles away in Clarkia. No drinking water is available at the garnet site so bring plenty of your own beverages.

OREGON

Gold Panning -
Wallowa - Whitman
National Forest
McCully Forks Campground

REGION:
Northwest

ADDRESS:
1550 Dewey Avenue
P.O. Box 907
Baker, Oregon 97814
(541) 523-6391

DIRECTION:
Take Interstate 84 to Baker City, Oregon (Exit 306). Proceed southwest on State Highway 7, bearing right onto County Road 410. In Sumpter, take County Road 520 approximately 7 miles to the mine. The mine is located on McCully Forks Creek just to the west of Sumpter.

SEASON:
Late spring to mid-fall

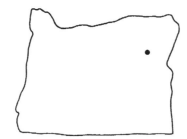

HOURS:
Daylight

COST:
Free

WHAT TO BRING:
Bring standard mining and gold mining equipment. Sluice boxes and dredges up to four inches are permitted. Bring your own food, camping supplies and drinking water. This is a national forest and camping is primitive.

INFORMATION:
This campground is on national forest property and is open for gold panning only. Gold is found on the riverbanks, around rocks and in the gravel deposits above the water line from the winter's high water runoff. The rangers ask that you be sure to let a friend know where you are camping, when you plan to be visiting and that you check back after your return.

In Oregon, areas below the vegetation line on rivers, streams and ocean beaches belong to the state of Oregon and are open for recreational gold panning. Don't disturb vegetation, control your fires, carry out your trash and take care of our public land.

OREGON

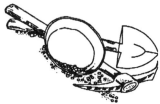

Gold Panning -
Wallowa - Whitman
National Forest
Deer Creek Campground

REGION:
Northwest

ADDRESS:
1550 Dewey Avenue
P.O. Box 907
Baker, Oregon 97814
(541) 523-6391

DIRECTIONS:
Take Interstate 84 to Baker City, Oregon (Exit 306). Proceed southwest on State Highway 7 until you get to County Road 656, just before the town of Sumpter. Turn right onto County Road 656 and travel approximately 3 miles to Deer Creek Campground.

SEASON:
Late spring to mid-fall

HOURS:
Daylight

COST:
Free

WHAT TO BRING:
Bring standard mining and gold mining equipment. Sluice boxes and dredges up to four inches are permitted. Bring your own food, camping supplies and drinking water. This is a national forest and camping is primitive.

INFORMATION:
This campground is on national forest property. Panning and dredging are permitted. Dredging requires a permit which can be obtained by calling the number above. Bring all your own supplies. Gold is found on the riverbanks, around rocks and in the gravel deposits above the water line from the winter's high water runoff.

The rangers ask that you be sure that you let a friend know where you are camping, when you plan to be visiting and that you check back with them upon your return. In Oregon, areas below the vegetation line on rivers, streams and ocean beaches belong to the state of Oregon and are open for recreational gold panning. Don't disturb vegetation, control your fires, carry out your trash and take care of our public land.

OREGON

Gold Panning - Wallowa - Whitman National Forest Antlers Campground

REGION:
Northwest

ADDRESS:
1550 Dewey Avenue
P.O. Box 907
Baker, Oregon 97814
(541) 523-6391

DIRECTIONS:
From Sumpter, Oregon, take State Highway 7 past National Forest Primary Road 656. Bear left staying on State Highway 7 where National Forest Primary Road 410 branches right. Drive approximately 8 miles. Then turn left onto County Road 529 to the Antlers Campground.

SEASON:
Late spring to mid-fall

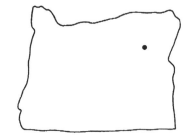

HOURS:
Daylight

COST:
Free

WHAT TO BRING:
Bring standard mining and gold mining equipment. Sluice boxes and dredges up to four inches are permitted. Bring your own food, camping supplies and drinking water. This is a national forest and camping is primitive.

INFORMATION:
    This campground is on national forest property. Panning and dredging are permitted. Dredging requires a permit which can be obtained by calling the number above. Bring all your own supplies. Gold is found on the riverbanks, around rocks and in the gravel above the water line deposited by the spring high water runoff.

    The rangers ask that you be sure that you let a friend know where you are camping, when you plan to be visiting and that you check back after your return. In Oregon, areas below the vegetation line on rivers, streams and ocean beaches belong to the state of Oregon and are open for recreational gold panning. Don't disturb vegetation, control your fires, carry out your trash and take care of our public land.

OREGON

*Gold Panning -
Wallowa - Whitman
National Forest
Eagle Forks Campground*

REGION:
Northwest

ADDRESS:
1550 Dewey Avenue
P.O. Box 907
Baker, Oregon 97814
(541) 523-6391

DIRECTION:
From Richland, Oregon, take Eagle Forks Drive north to New Bridge, Oregon. Continue through New Bridge, Oregon, on Eagle Forks Drive north (National Forest Scenic Route 7735) approximately 9 miles to Eagle Forks Campground. The campground phone number is (541) 742-7511.

SEASON:
Late spring to mid-fall

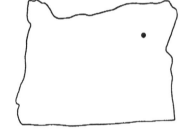

HOURS:
Daylight

COST:
Free

WHAT TO BRING:
Bring standard mining and gold mining equipment. Sluice boxes and dredges up to four inches are permitted. Bring your own food, camping supplies and drinking water. This is a national forest and camping is primitive.

INFORMATION:
This campground is on national forest property. Panning and dredging are permitted. Dredging requires a permit which can be obtained by calling the number above. Bring all your own supplies. Gold is found on the riverbanks, around rocks and in the gravel deposits above the water line from the winter's high water runoff.

The rangers ask that you be sure that you let a friend know where you are camping, when you plan to be visiting and that you check back after your return. In Oregon, areas below the vegetation line on rivers, streams and ocean beaches belong to the state of Oregon and are open for recreational gold panning. Don't disturb vegetation, control your fires, carry out your trash and take care of our public land.

OREGON

Thundereggs & Jaspers - White Fir Springs

REGION:
Northwest

ADDRESS:
Prineville Chamber of Commerce
390 North Fairview
Prineville, Oregon 97754
(541) 447-6304

DIRECTIONS:
From Prineville take U.S. Highway 26 to milepost 41. Turn left on Forest Service Road 3350 and continue 5 miles to the Chamber of Commerce claim sign.

SEASON:
Open all year round, weather permitting

HOUR:
Daylight

COST:
Free

WHAT TO BRING:
You will need rock hammers, picks, shovels, a bucket, safety goggles and gloves.

INFORMATION:
White Fir thundereggs are made up of an agatized jasper composition with a rhyolite matrix. They occur in many colors and combinations of brown, tan, yellow, red and mauve. The thundereggs range in size from one-quarter inch in diameter to five feet in diameter. Thundereggs are geodes which are round rock bubbles formed by gases. The outside of the rock is ordinary; the inside is filled with agate or jasper.

The Chamber of Commerce maintains several claims in the area. Be sure to stay on the chamber's claim, which is marked. Leave the gates as you found them. If the gates are open, leave them open; if closed, close them again after you leave. Please don't litter. This is an open area, not a private mine, so you need to bring all your own tools.

OREGON

Jasper Thundereggs - Whistler Springs

REGION:
Northwest

ADDRESS:
Prineville Chamber of Commerce
390 North Fairview
Prineville, Oregon 97754
(541) 447-6304

DIRECTIONS:
From Prineville, travel east on U.S. Highway 26 to milepost 49 and 50. Turn left after the sign reading Bandit Springs and travel 6 miles on Forest Service Road 27. At Forest Service Road 500 turn right and drive a short distance to Whistler Springs.

SEASON:
Open all year round, weather permitting

HOURS:
Daylight

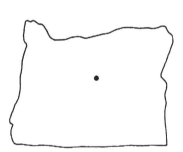

COST:
Free

WHAT TO BRING:
You need standard mining tools. This is an open area, not a private mine, so you need to bring all your own tools.

INFORMATION:
   Thundereggs at the Whistler Springs area have been found in blue, carnelian, plume and moss colors of agatized jasper. Many eggs' cross sections appear to resemble seascapes, animal pictures and other formations within the rock. This area is heavily worked and rocks may be more difficult to find.
   A thunderegg may be a nodular, solid sphere of rock or a hollow rock (geode). Geodes may hide beautiful crystals within. These eggs have a brown or russet-colored outer shell that may be knobby or ribbed. The inner shell may have a thin or intermediate lining of iron or manganese, occasionally quartz or opal. The center is usually quartz with or without inclusions, pattern growth or crystals. Opal interiors are rare but do occur. Plume patterns also occur and are valuable finds. Rock sizes range from less than an inch to five feet in diameter. Most specimens are the size of baseballs.
   Stop by the Prineville Chamber of Commerce for a free map of the area. Maps are also available at the Forest Service Office.

OREGON

Thundereggs & Agates - Richardson's Recreational Ranch

REGION:
Northwest

ADDRESS:
Gateway Route, Box 440
Madras, Oregon 97741
(800) 433-2680

DIRECTIONS:
From Madras, Oregon take U.S. Highway 97 north 11 miles. Turn right at milepost marker 81 on U.S. Highway 97 and travel 3 miles to the ranch office.

SEASON:
Open daily, weather permitting

HOURS:
Office hours: 7:00 a.m. to 5:00 p.m.

COST:
50¢ per pound of material you dig yourself.

WHAT TO BRING:
The ranch provides free use of rock picks. You will need gloves, rock hammers, buckets, chisels and wedges to do any hard rock mining. You can do without tools if you plan to search the tailings piles.

INFORMATION:
   Richardson's Recreational Ranch is famous for its thundereggs. They range in size from one-quarter inch in diameter to five feet in diameter. Thundereggs are geodes which are round rock bubbles formed by gases. The outside of the rock is ordinary. The inside is filled with agate or jasper and in some cases crystals. Other rocks found here include moss agate, jasper, jasp-agate, and Oregon sunset and rainbow agates.
   The Thundereggs received their name from Native American legend. They were said to be the eggs of the Thunderbird gods and used by other gods as weapons.
   The area is very scenic, so bring your camera. Camping without hookups and showers are free to camping customers.

OREGON

Soapstone & Gold Panning - Rogue River National Forest, Little Applegate Recreation Area

REGION:
Northwest

ADDRESS:
Applegate Ranger Station
6941 Upper Applegate Road
Jacksonville, Oregon 97530
(541) 899-1812

DIRECTIONS:
Applegate Recreation Area and Rogue River National Forest are located 14.5 miles south of Jacksonville, Oregon. Take State Highway 238, west of Medford, through Jacksonville to Ruch, Oregon. Turn right onto Applegate Road/National Forest Primary Road 10 for 2 miles. Cross the Little Applegate River and turn left onto Little Applegate Road.

SEASON:
Open all year round

HOURS:
Daylight

COST:
Panning: $1.00 per day
Dredging: $5.00 per day

WHAT TO BRING:
Bring standard mining and gold mining equipment. Sluice boxes and dredges up to four inches are permitted. Bring your own food, camping supplies and drinking water. This is a national forest and camping is primitive.

INFORMATION:
    Rock collecting is a popular activity in this national forest. Soapstone is found throughout the district, but much of it is under claim. Soapstone is white to green and feels greasy to the touch. It is soft and easily carved, used in cosmetics, talc, sculpture and as an electrical insulator. Quartz and green serpentinized peridotite are also collected throughout the area, but are not concentrated in one location. Copper and red cinnabar are found here but are rare.
    Jacksonville was a gold boom town. In the 1850s when the gold ran out, it became a copper and cinnabar mining town. Jacksonville is on the National Registry of Historic Places with many buildings dating back to the 1800s. Mining permits for the Oregon territory of the national forest are available at the ranger station.

OREGON

Gold Panning - Rogue River National Forest, Tunnel Ridge Recreation Area

REGION:
Northwest

ADDRESS:
Bureau of Land Management
Medford District Office
3040 Biddle Road
Medford, Oregon 97504
(541) 770-2200

DIRECTIONS:
Tunnel Ridge Recreation Area is located on State Highway 238, west of Medford. Go through Jacksonville to Ruch. Turn right onto Applegate Road for 2 miles. Cross the Little Applegate River and turn left onto Little Applegate Road.

SEASON:
Open all year round
Dredging June 15 to September 15

HOURS:
8:00 a.m. to 6:00 p.m.

COST:
$1.00 per day

WHAT TO BRING:
Bring standard mining and gold mining equipment. Sluice boxes and dredges up to four inches are permitted. Bring your own food, camping supplies and drinking water. This is a national forest and camping is primitive.

INFORMATION:
This area has two spots in close proximity to search for gold—Tunnel Ridge and, upstream, Little Applegate. If you plan to dredge you must obtain a permit by calling the number listed above. The sites are open year round for panning and from June 15 to September 15 for dredging. Dredges can be operated from 9:00 a.m. to 6:00 p.m. Digging into or undermining the stream and riverbanks is not permitted.

Camping is permitted free for up to 14 days in the primitive sites. Both sites charge a dollar a day to pan for gold. These areas have produced gold and have good potential.

OREGON

Gold Panning - Rogue River National Forest, Gold Nugget Recreation Area

REGION:
Northwest

ADDRESS:
Bureau of Land Management
Medford District Office, 3040 Biddle Road
Medford, Oregon 97504
(541) 770-2200

DIRECTIONS:
From Medford, take Interstate 5 northwest to Gold Hill, Oregon. Take State Highway 234 north approximately 2 miles and look for signs for the Gold Nugget Recreation Area.

SEASON:
Open all year round
Dredging June 15 to September 15

HOURS:
8:00 a.m. to 6:00 p.m.

COST:
$1.00 per day

WHAT TO BRING:
Bring standard mining and gold mining equipment. Sluice boxes and dredges up to four inches are permitted. Bring your own food, camping supplies and drinking water. This is a national forest and camping is primitive.

INFORMATION:
Located east of Grants Pass, Oregon, on the Rogue River, the Gold Nugget Recreation Area is maintained by the Bureau of Land Management. This area is supported by your tax dollars and is available for your use.

If you plan to dredge you must obtain a permit by calling the number listed above. The sites are open year round for panning and from June 15 to September 15 for dredging. Dredges can be operated from 9:00 a.m. to 6:00 p.m. Digging into or undermining the stream and riverbanks is not permitted.

Camping is permitted free for up to 14 days in the primitive sites. Both sites charge a dollar a day to pan for gold. These areas have produced gold and have good potential.

OREGON

Gold Panning - Sharps Creek Recreation Area

REGION:
Northwest

ADDRESS:
2890 Chad Drive
P.O. Box 10226
Eugene, Oregon 97440
(541) 683-6600

DIRECTIONS:
From Cottage Grove, Oregon, head east on Row River Road. Travel 15 miles. Row River Road becomes Shoreline Drive. Travel approximately 12 miles to Sharps Creek Road. Turn right onto Sharps Creek Road at the sign for the Sharps Creek Recreation Area. Drive 3 miles to the site.

SEASON:
Open June to November for prospecting
Camping open May 15 to November 15 (10 sites)

HOURS:
Daylight

COST:
Free to prospect
Camping — $5.00 per site

WHAT TO BRING:
Bring standard mining and gold mining equipment. Sluice boxes and dredges up to four inches are permitted. Bring your own food, supplies and drinking water.

INFORMATION:
Sharps Creek Recreation Area allows gold panning and dredging after the fish spawning season which is March 1 to May 31. Dredging requires a permit which can be obtained by calling the Department of Environmental Quality at (503) 378-8240.

The district office asks you to be conscious of other recreational users. If people are swimming in this popular area, please set up your dredge or sluicing equipment downstream of swimmers. Many areas along the stream are private claims so be sure to stay within the recreational area boundaries. The district office will provide you with a map for a small fee, which will help you stay off private claims.

The campground is open between May 15 and November 15. Camping is limited to 14 days. Sites are primitive.

OREGON

Gold Panning - Quartzville Recreational Corridor, Dogwood Recreation Site

REGION:
Northwest

ADDRESS:
2890 Chad Drive
P.O. Box 10226
Eugene, Oregon 97440
(541) 683-6600

DIRECTIONS:
Sweet Home, Oregon, is slightly northeast of Eugene, Oregon. From Sweet Home travel northeast on Quartzville Access Road past Green Peter Reservoir. The Dogwood Recreation Site is 22 miles from Sweet Home.

SEASON:
Open all year round
Dredging from July 1 to September 1 only

HOURS:
Daylight

COST:
Free

WHAT TO BRING:
Bring standard mining and gold mining equipment. Sluice boxes and dredges up to four inches are permitted. Bring your own food, camping supplies and drinking water. This is a national forest and camping is primitive.

INFORMATION:
Quartzville Corridor has been producing gold since the 1800s. In the 1860s Quartzville was a tent city of gold miners. Gold panning and dredging are permitted. Dredging requires a permit which can be obtained by calling the Department of Environmental Quality at (503) 378-8240. Keep all mining activity inside the ten-mile Quartzville Recreational Corridor. This location should produce some gold and is a beautiful area of the country.

Camping is permitted in the Dogwood Recreation Site and seven miles north at the Yellowbottom Recreation Site. The camping is primitive and on a first come, first served basis. No reservations are accepted. Camping is limited to 14 days. Quartzville's campgrounds are also nearby and charge a small fee.

OREGON

*Agates & Jaspers -
Oregon's Ocean Beaches*

REGION:
Northwest

ADDRESS:
U.S. 101 — north of Newport
No phone

DIRECTIONS:
The best spot for collecting agates is on Agate Beach on the Oregon Coast, just north of Newport on U.S. Highway 101.

SEASON:
Open all year

HOURS:
Daylight

COST:
Free

WHAT TO BRING:
You need a container or pail to carry your agates. The Pacific ocean is COLD, so you may want to wear rubber boots.

INFORMATION:
    This beach lies at the mouth of Big Creek, which carries the agates down from northeast of Newport, Oregon. Agate Beach Wayside is a pull-off for your day use of these beaches. This blacktop parking area has clean restrooms and a tunnel under Ocean Drive (U.S. 101) to the beach.
    Agates have a smooth, glassy feel. They are found in many earth colors and the rock surface may have an orange-peel texture. Agates may appear translucent; jaspers are opaque. Agates and jaspers are easier to spot when they are wet. On the beach you will see some small streams which outlet to the ocean. Streambeds and wet sandy beaches are good places to search. Local rock shops sell the beach agates and jasper in their natural form and the polished variety. Local artists have also made some beautiful jewelry from the stones.

WASHINGTON

Gold Panning - Sullivan Creek in Colville National Forest

REGION:
Northwest

ADDRESS:
Sullivan Lake Ranger District
12641 Sullivan Lake Road
Metaline Falls, Washington 99153
(509) 446-7500

SEASON:
Open all year round

HOURS:
Daylight

COST:
Free

DIRECTIONS:
Metaline Falls is approximately 90 miles north of Spokane, Washington. From Metaline Falls, take Sullivan Lake Road 8 miles to the prospecting area on Sullivan Creek. The creek is within the Sullivan Lake Ranger District in the Colville National Forest. Begin at the Sullivan Creek ranger station for directions and information on the creek.

WHAT TO BRING:

Bring standard mining and gold mining equipment. Sluice boxes and dredges (two-and-one-half to four-inch dredges, depending on area) are permitted. Bring your own food, camping supplies and drinking water. This is a national forest and camping is primitive.

INFORMATION:

There are two areas, or reaches, to be prospected and gold of all sizes can be found here. The upper reach extends from the creek's source to its junction with Outlet Creek near Sullivan Creek Ranger Station. This area is open for dredging and sluicing from July 1 to August 31. Dredges up to two and one-half inches in diameter are permitted. The lower reach area is located between the junction of Outlet and Sullivan Creeks to Pend Oreille River, which is north of Metaline Falls. This area is open from June 1 to October 31 each year.

Dredges up to four inches in diameter are permitted in the lower reaches. Gold panning is permitted in both areas year round. A permit is required to dredge. It can be obtained from the Washington State Department of Fisheries and Wildlife, Habitat Management, Olympia Headquarters Office, 600 North Capitol Way, Olympia, Washington 98501-1091. The phone number is (360) 902-2200.

ALASKA

Gold Panning - Nome Creek

REGION:
Northwest

ADDRESS:
Bureau of Land Management
Steese/White Mountain District Office
1150 University Ave.
Fairbanks, Alaska 99709
Public Lands Info. Center (907) 456-0527

DIRECTIONS:
From Fairbanks, Alaska take Steese Highway (6) northeast 57.3 miles. Then travel north for 6 miles on U.S. Creek Road. Large white signs mark the specific 4 mile stretch of Nome Creek open to public mining.

SEASON:
May to October

HOURS:
Daylight
(In the summer daylight is 24 hours a day.)

COST:
Free

WHAT TO BRING:
Only hand tools such as gold pans, prybars, picks, shovels, manually-fed sluice boxes and rocker boxes are permitted.

INFORMATION:
There is a four-mile section along Nome Creek that is open to gold panning. Access to the public claim area requires one ford of Nome Creek. Call the Public Lands Information Center at the above number for current road conditions. The public claim area is clearly marked with large white signs located along the creek. Stay within this area to insure that you do not trespass on private claims.

Gold panning and prospecting are permitted, with some restrictions, on most public land in Alaska. These lands include national forests, wildlife refuges, and some state parks. You can get information on additional areas to prospect in Alaska by contacting the Alaska Public Lands Information Center at the number listed above.

ALASKA

Gold -
Paradise Valley

REGION:
Northwest

ADDRESS:
Paradise Valley
3350 Thomas Street, #165
Fairbanks, Alaska 99709
(907) 479-5704

DIRECTIONS:
Arrival may be by car or plane. By plane you will fly to Fairbanks, Alaska, then fly from Fairbanks to Paradise Valley. Paradise Valley is 230 miles north/northwest of Fairbanks.

By car, you will travel through Yukon Territory, Canada, and then to Alaska. There are several route options. Paradise Valley will help you with your route.

SEASON:
The middle of May through September

HOURS:
Daylight (In the summer daylight is 24 hours a day.)

COST:
Metal detecting — $120.00
Gold panning — $80.00
Sluicing — $90.00
Dredging (2 1/2") — $130.00
Dredging (3") — $150.00

WHAT TO BRING:
Prospecting equipment is available to rent or bring your own. Paradise Valley will provide you with a list of clothing, food and other supplies needed for your trip.

INFORMATION:
Paradise Valley produces some of the largest gold nuggets found today. They are a full-service wilderness recreation company with 20-years experience. You are lodged in a 12' x 24' or larger wood cabin. Send your own food prior to your trip. Usually people stop at the grocery store in Fairbanks to pick up their food prior to arrival. Food can be arranged for $50.00 per day, additional charge.

You must book ahead to visit Paradise Valley. No dogs are allowed and no hunting. If you are not prospecting but visiting with a prospector, the cost is $75.00 per day. This is a trip of a lifetime.

GLOSSARY OF TERMS

ADMIRALTY CLAIM: A specific type of claim leased to salvaging companies to guarantee their exclusive use of a certain area of ocean bottom. This means you may not use a metal detector in the area of the wreck sites.

BACK HOE: Large machine similar to a bulldozer, which moves dirt and uncovers new material to mine.

BLACK SAND: Black grains of sand made of hematite. This is a very heavy metal that is often associated with gold. Seeing it in your gold pan is a good sign.

BUREAU OF LAND MANAGEMENT (BLM): National organization created to protect, preserve and manage public land. Some mining and rock collecting is permitted on BLM land in designated areas. Permits are often required.

CARAT: The unit used to express the weight of gemstones. One carat is equal to 200 milligrams.

CLAIMS: A tract of land staked out by an individual to mine. This means it is not open to you and is protected by law.

CONCENTRATES: Dirt that has been reduced by removing all large rocks, light soil and organic material. This leaves just concentrated, heavy dirt that is likely to contain heavy gold, or gemstones.

DISCRIMINATOR: A function of a metal detector, used to tune out junk metal such as flip tops and tin foil. It is also used to tune out mineralized soil or rocks (hot rocks).

DREDGE: Mining equipment used in a stream to find gold. It works like a powerful water vacuum on the streambed. It sucks up the bottom soil. Heavy material including gold falls onto a ridged mat, while light material washes through and falls back to the stream floor.

DUMP: Where the non-valuable rock and debris is discarded at a mine site.

ESCUDO: Spanish coin made of gold. An escudo weighs one ounce. They are also commonly called a doubloon. They were minted in South America by the Spanish conquistadors from the 1600s to the 1700s. Gold was then shipped to Spain. Some treasure galleons were lost in storms along the U.S. coast.

GOLD DUST: Fine particles of gold found in rivers, streams, oceans, soil and, hopefully, your gold pan. Finding gold dust indicates you have a found a good place to search more thoroughly.

HAND-OPERATED TOOLS: Tools used by hand. Some examples include shovels, picks, garden trowels, garden rakes and pry bars.

HIGH BANKER: This is a desert sluice box. It is used in places where water is unavailable or inconvenient. It has its own supply of recycled water that wets dirt and sends it into a sluice box. Some high bankers use hot air instead of water.

HOT ROCKS: Rocks with a concentration of metal or salt that cause metal detectors to give a false signal. This signal leads metal detectors to think they have found something of value. Hot rocks should be checked. If quartz is found you may have hope that gold may still be present.

MESH SCREENS: Mesh screens are used to remove larger rocks and organic material from dirt in an effort to concentrate it. Mesh screens are commercially produced and easily fit into five-gallon buckets. Many miners make their own with chicken wire and wood. Sizes describe the size of the mesh openings. The most common sizes are quarter-inch and half-inch mesh screens.

MINE RUN: A large quantity of mined material offered for sale. It may include as much material as is produced in a half day or full day of mining. The quantity of material included varies from mine to mine, so get specifics before you buy.

MINERALIZATION: Soil that has a concentration of minerals, metals or salts. This plays havoc with metal detectors which read it as valuable material such as gold or silver. Rocks may also be mineralized and are called hot rocks. Wet ocean sand is highly mineralized. A metal detector with a good discriminator is needed in cases of mineralized material.

MINI JIG: A mining tool that washes dirt and removes light waste rock and organic material. The condensed material containing heavier metal is collected for more careful inspection. It is used to find such materials as garnets, gold, rubies and sapphires.

NATIVE ROCK: The rock most prevalent to a specific area. The rock surrounding or being penetrated by mineral veins and deposits.

PLACER GOLD: Gold found in its natural state without any host rock. Examples include gold dust and gold nuggets. Placer gold is commonly found in streams and rivers where it has washed away from its source.

PRY BAR: A tool made of steel that is used to move a heavy rock or to turn over a rock to expose material underneath. A crow bar is a large pry bar. They come in a variety of sizes.

REALE: A Spanish coin made of silver. A one-ounce coin was called an eight reale. This is where the term "pieces of eight" came from. They were minted in South America by the Spanish from the 1600s to the 1700s. Some treasure galleons were lost in storms along the U.S. coast.

ROCKHOUND: What you are if you bought this book. Otherwise known as a person who enjoys finding, collecting, and cutting different kinds of rocks.

SEEDED: This is dirt offered to you by a mine that has had objects added to it to ensure that you are not disappointed. Material added is not always indigenous to the area. Gemstones added are usually of inferior quality.

SLUICE BOX: This piece of mining equipment is used in combination with a running stream. The water runs through one end of the box and out the other. Material from the streambed is added to the top of the box. Light material runs off with the water, while the gold and heavy materials fall to the mat in the sluice box for closer examination.

SNUFFER BOTTLE: A plastic bottle used to suck up fine gold dust from your gold pan.

TAILINGS: Term referring to mining material that has been discarded during the mining process, also called waste rock. This is not usually the best material to search, but can contain fine specimens and is much easier than digging your own.

ULTRAVIOLET LIGHT: A type of light bulb that is long or short wave. It is also called a black light. This light is used to spot rocks that fluoresce, or glow in a variety of colors as the ultraviolet light is shone upon them.

UNDER CLAIM: Area of land that has been claimed by an individual or company to mine. This means it is not open to you and is protected by law. Claim markers mean keep off and should be respected.

BIBLIOGRAPHY

Gold Prospectors Association of America. *1994 Gold Prospector's Mining Guide,* Temecula, California, 1994.

Mitchell, James R. *Gem Trails of Colorado,* Gem Guides Book Co., Baldwin Park, California, 1997.

Mitchell, James R. *Gem Trails of Nevada,* Gem Guides Book Co., Baldwin Park, California, 1991.

Mitchell, James R. *Gem Trails of New Mexico,* Gem Guides Book Co., Baldwin Park, California, 1996.

Petralia, Joseph, F. *GOLD!, GOLD!, A Beginner's Handbook and Recreational Guide.* Sierra Trading Post, San Francisco, California, 1980.

Reilly, Kevin; Rowe, Gary T; and Marnville, Kevin. *Hurricane Treasure, 1715 Beach Sites, Locations Revealed,* Pirate Express Publishing, Pompano Beach, Florida, 1990.

SUGGESTED READING

Magazines

Lapidary Journal
60 Chesnut Ave., Suite 201
Devon, PA 19333-1312

Rock & Gem
2660 E. Main Street
Ventura, CA 93003

Rocks & Minerals
Heldref Publications
4000 Albemarle Street, N.W.
Washington, D.C. 20016

Books

IDENTIFYING ROCKS & MINERALS

Arem, Joel. *Rocks and Minerals.* Geoscience Press, Tucson, AZ, 1974.

Chesterman, Charles W. *Audubon Field Guide to North American Rocks and Minerals.* Alfred A. Knopf, Inc., New York, 1979.

Fejer, Eva and Cecelia Fitzsimons. *An Instant Guide to Rocks and Minerals.* Crescent Books, New York, 1988.

Horenstein, Sidney, editor. *Simon & Schuster's Guide to Fossils.* Simon & Schuster Inc., New York, 1986.

Maley, Terry S. *Field Geology Illustrated.* Mineral Land Publications, Boise, ID, 1994.

Pellant, Chris. *Eyewitness Handbooks: Rocks and Minerals.* Dorling Kindersley, Ltd., London, 1992.

Pough, Frederick H. *Petersen Field Guides® Rocks and Minerals,* 5th ed. Houghton Mifflin Co., New York, 1996.

Pough, Frederick H. *Petersen First Guide® Rocks and Minerals.* Houghton Mifflin Co., New York, 1988.

Prinz, Martin, George Harlow, and Joseph Peters, editors. *Simon & Schuster's Guide to Rocks and Minerals.* Simon & Schuster Inc., New York, 1977.

Zim, Herbert S. and Paul R. Shaffer. *Rocks and Minerals.* Western Publishing Co., Inc., Racine, WI, 1957.

FIELD COLLECTING

Blair, Gerry. *Rockhounding Arizona.* Falcon Press, Helena, MT, 1992.

Butler, Gail A. *The Rockhound's Guide to California.* Falcon Press, Helena, MT, 1995.

Crow, Melinda. *The Rockhound's Guide to Texas.* Falcon Press, Helena, MT, 1994.

Ettinger, L. J. *Rockhound and Prospector's Bible,* 3d ed. L. J. Ettinger, Reno, NV, 1992.

Feldman, Robert. *The Rockhound's Guide to Montana.* Falcon Press, Helena, MT, 1985.

Girard, Roselle M. *Texas Rocks and Minerals: An Amateur's Guide,* rev. ed. Bureau of Economic Geology, University of Texas, Austin, TX, 1964.

Johnson, H. Cyril and Robert N. Johnson. *Coast to Coast Gem Atlas,* 4th ed. Cy Johnson & Son, Susanville, CA, 1987.

Kimbler, Frank S., and Robert J. Narsavage, Jr. *New Mexico Rocks and Minerals.* Sunstone Press, Santa Fe, NM, 1981.

Krause, Barry. *Mineral Collector's Handbook.* Sterling Publishing Co., Inc., New York, 1996.

Mitchell, James R. *Gem Trails of Arizona.* Gem Guides Book Co., Baldwin Park, CA, 1995.

Mitchell, James R. *Gem Trails of Colorado.* Gem Guides Book Co., Baldwin Park, CA, 1997.

Mitchell, James R. *Gem Trails of Nevada.* Gem Guides Book Co., Baldwin Park, CA, 1991.

Mitchell, James R. *Gem Trails of New Mexico.* Gem Guides Book Co., Baldwin Park, CA, 1996.

SUGGESTED READING cont.

Mitchell, James R. *Gem Trails of Northern California.* Gem Guides Book Co., Baldwin Park, CA, 1995.

Mitchell, James R. *Gem Trails of Oregon.* Gem Guides Book Co., Baldwin Park, CA, 1997.

Mitchell, James R. *Gem Trails of Southern California.* Gem Guides Book Co., Baldwin Park, CA, 1996.

Mitchell, James R. *Gem Trails of Texas.* Gem Guides Book Co., Baldwin Park, CA, 1987.

Mitchell, James R. *Gem Trails of Utah.* Gem Guides Book Co., Baldwin Park, CA, 1996.

Mitchell, James R. *The Rockhound's Handbook.* Gem Guides Book Co., Baldwin Park, CA, 1997.

Ream, Lanny R. *Gems and Minerals of Washington.* Jackson Mountain Press, Renton, WA, 1990.

Ream, Lanny R. *Idaho Minerals.* L. R. Ream Publishing, Coeur d'Alene, ID, 1989.

Sanborn, William B. *Handbook of Crystal and Mineral Collecting.* Gem Guides Book Co., Baldwin Park, CA, 1987.

Sinkankas, John. *Gemstone and Mineral Data Book.* Van Nostrand Reinhold, New York, 1981.

Sinkankas, John. *Field Collecting Gemstones and Minerals.* Geoscience Press, Phoenix, AZ, 1988.

Stepanski, Scott, and Karenne Snow. *Gem Trails of Pennsylvania and New Jersey.* Gem Guides Book Co., Baldwin Park, CA, 1996.

Voynick, Stephen M. *Colorado Rockhounding.* Mountain Press Publishing Company, Missoula, MT, 1994.

Wilson, James R. *A Collector's Guide to Rock, Mineral & Fossil Localities of Utah.* Utah Geological Survey, Salt Lake City, UT, 1995.

Zeitner, June Culp. *Midwest Gem, Fossil and Mineral Trails: Great Lakes States.* Gem Guides Book Co., Baldwin Park, CA, 1988.

Zeitner, June Culp. *Midwest Gem, Fossil and Mineral Trails: Prairie States.* Gem Guides Book Co., Baldwin Park, CA, 1989.

GOLD PROSPECTING

Basque, Garnet. *Gold Panner's Manual.* Heritage House Publishing Co., Ltd., Surry, B.C., 1991.

Basque, Garnet. *Methods of Placer Mining.* Sunfire Publications, Ltd., Langly, B.C., 1994.

Black, Jack. *Gold Prospector's Handbook.* Gem Guides Book Co., Baldwin Park, CA, 1978.

de Lorenzo, Lois. *Gold Fever: The Art of Panning and Sluicing.* Gem Guides Book Co., Baldwin Park, CA, 1978.
Garrett, Charles L. *Modern Metal Detectors,* Rev. ed. Ram Publishing Company, Dallas, TX, 1995.

Gintzler, A. S. *Rough & Ready Prospectors,* (Ages 6-12). John Muir Publications, Santa Fe, NM, 1994.

Klein, James and Jerry Keene. *How to Find Gold.* Keene Engineering Co., Northridge, CA, 1996.

Lagal, Roy. *The New Gold Panning is Easy.* Ram Publishing Company, Dallas, TX, 1992.

McCracken, Dave. *Gold Mining in the 1990's.* Keene Industries, Northridge, CA, 1993.

Ryan, A. H. *The Weekend Gold Miner.* Gem Guides Book Co., Baldwin Park, CA, 1991.

FIELD NOTES

FIELD NOTES

FIELD NOTES

FIELD NOTES

HAVE WE MISSED A MINE OR COLLECTING SITE?

If you know of a mine or collecting site that should be included in future editions of this book, please bring it to our attention. Just fill out the bottom half of this sheet and return it to the address listed below. If your location is added to the next edition, we will send you a copy of the new book free. Thank you for your help.

- -

Name of Mine: _____

Address: _____

_____

_____

_____

Phone: _____

Type of Material Found at Mine: _____

_____

Method of Collecting: _____
(Equipment Used) _____

Cost: _____ Season of Operation: _____

Additional Information: _____

_____

_____

Your Name & Address: _____

_____

_____

Return to: Editor
Gem Guides Book Co.
315 Cloverleaf Drive, Suite F
Baldwin Park, CA 91706